Better Homes and Gardens®
grilling

familydinners

Better Homes and Gardens.
grilling
familydinners

This book is printed on acid-free paper.

Copyright © 2011 by Meredith Corporation, Des Moines, IA. All rights reserved.

Published by World Publications Group, 140 Laurel Street, East Bridgewater, MA 02333, www.wrldpub.com

No part of this publication may be reproduced, stored in a retrieval system, or transmitted in any form or by any means, electronic, mechanical, photocopying, recording, scanning, or otherwise, except as permitted under Section 107 or 108 of the 1976 United States Copyright Act, without either the prior written permission of the Publisher, or authorization through payment of the appropriate per-copy fee to the Copyright Clearance Center, Inc., 222 Rosewood Drive, Danvers, MA 01923, (978) 750–8400, fax (978) 750-4470, or on the web at www.copyright.com. Requests to the Publisher for permission should be addressed to the Permissions Department, John Wiley & Sons, Inc., 111 River Street, Hoboken, NJ 07030, (201) 748–6011, fax (201) 748–6008, or online at http://www.wiley.com/go/permissions.

Limit of Liability/Disclaimer of Warranty: While the publisher and author have used their best efforts in preparing this book, they make no representations or warranties with respect to the accuracy or completeness of the contents of this book and specifically disclaim any implied warranties of merchantability or fitness for a particular purpose. No warranty may be created or extended by sales representatives or written sales materials. The advice and strategies contained herein may not be suitable for your situation. You should consult with a professional where appropriate. Neither the publisher nor author shall be liable for any loss of profit or any other commercial damages, including but not limited to special, incidental, consequential, or other damages.

Library of Congress Cataloging-in-Publication Data

Better homes and gardens grilling family dinners.
    p. cm.
  Includes index.
  ISBN 978-1-57215-692-0 (cloth); 978-1-57215-739-2 (cloth) -- ISBN 978-1-57215-693-7 (pbk.)
 1. Barbecuing. 2. Broiling. 3. Cookbooks. I. Better homes and gardens. II. Title: Grilling family dinners.
  TX840.B3B47 2011
  641.7'6--dc22
                                        2010042875

Printed in China.

10 9 8 7 6 5 4 3 2 1

Better Homes and Gardens® Test Kitchen

Our seal assures you that every recipe in *Grilling Family Dinners* has been tested in the Better Homes and Gardens Test Kitchen®. This means that each recipe is practical and reliable and meets our high standards of taste appeal. We guarantee your satisfaction with this book for as long as you own it.

contents

Ready, Set, Grill! 6

Just for Starters 10

Burgers, Sandwiches, and Wraps 34

Chicken and Turkey 74

Pork 98

Ribs 120

Beef 136

Fish and Seafood 158

Simply Smokin' 184

On the Side 204

Metric Information 234

Index 235

ready, set, grill!

Cooking over glowing coals

should be easy and carefree. Just follow these guidelines so your grill and coals are ready to go.

FIRE UP!

Whether you grill with charcoal or gas, setting up the grill is easy.

For a charcoal grill:

About 25 to 30 minutes before cooking, remove the grill cover and open all the vents. Place the briquettes on the lower charcoal grate.

For **direct cooking,** use enough briquettes to cover the charcoal grate completely with one layer. Then pile these briquettes in a pyramid in the center of the grate.

For **indirect cooking,** the number of briquettes you need is based on your grill size. Check out the chart below.

Grill diameter in inches	Briquettes needed to start	Briquettes to add if coals start to cool during longer grill times
26¾	60	18
22½	50	16
18½	32	10

Light the coals as described in "Lighting the Coals," page 8, and let them burn until they are lightly covered with gray ash. Using long-handle tongs, arrange the coals according to the cooking method you want to use.

For **direct cooking,** spread the coals evenly across the bottom of the grill so the coals reach 3 inches beyond all sides of the food you will cook.

For **indirect cooking,** arrange coals at one side of the grill; place a drip pan on the other side. Or place the drip pan in the center of the grill and arrange coals into two piles on opposite sides of the pan. Install the grill rack and check the temperature.

For a gas grill:

Open the lid. Turn on the gas valve and turn the burners to high. Ignite as directed by the manufacturer. Close the lid and preheat the grill (usually with all burners on high for 10 to 15 minutes).

For **indirect cooking,** turn off the burners below where the food will grill. For direct cooking and indirect cooking, adjust burner controls to the temperature needed for cooking.

strive for the best flavor

More often than not, if you have spent time over a grill you have developed your own methodology and grilling techniques. Some are secrets to success, and others are ingredients to failure. Here are a few tried-and-true tricks to help you correct your grilling blunders or continue your achievements at the grill.

Use quality meat. Make sure your steaks are thick and well-marbled. The streaks of fat create wonderful, juicy flavor in meat, but be sure to trim large amounts of visible fat from around the outer edges of the meat. This reduces the dripping grease that causes flare-ups.

Pat meat dry. Pat meat dry with paper towels to eliminate all moisture on the meat's surface; otherwise, you will boil and braise your meat instead of grilling it.

Use fresh herbs. Throw a few sprigs of fresh thyme or rosemary over the coals just before you remove food from the grill. Or use an herb bouquet to baste your meat and veggies with sauce, giving them an added flavor punch.

Marinate. Marinades don't need to be complicated. Simply use a store-bought salad dressing or blend a few ingredients found in your spice rack and fridge. Combine juice, wine or other alcohol, fresh herbs, spices, garlic, onion, and peppers. Marinate the meat or poultry in a nonaluminum container to prevent off-flavors.

Add wood chunks and chips. The wood you choose—apple, cherry, hickory, oak, or other—is a matter of preference. Each type imparts a subtle smoky flavor to the meat. Think of smoke as a spice; too much of a good thing ruins the meal. Start off with a minimal amount of wood, and never add wood during the last half of grilling time.

Don't poke the meat. As tempting as it is to poke, mash, and play with meat while it grills, each poke only causes flavor and moisture loss as the juices drip to the bottom of the grill.

Don't flip your food too soon. Allow adequate time to sear the food before you move it from one spot to the other. Searing gives the food its rich caramelized color and flavor.

Let meat stand. Cutting into meat immediately after it's pulled from the grill causes all the flavorful juices to run out onto the plate. Let your meat stand 5 to 10 minutes to allow the meat to absorb its flavorful components.

testing doneness

Many factors help determine the amount of time needed to grill a given food. Direct grilling requires a lot less time than indirect grilling, but it also requires that you take your food off the grill at the right time. Factors that affect the amount of time needed to grill a food include the outside temperature, the food thickness, the food temperature, the desired doneness, and other conditions. Use the poke test to help you determine when your meat is done. Mimic the movements, below, and gently poke the fleshy section at the base of your thumb. The tension in your hand should match that of the meat, giving you a good indication of its doneness.

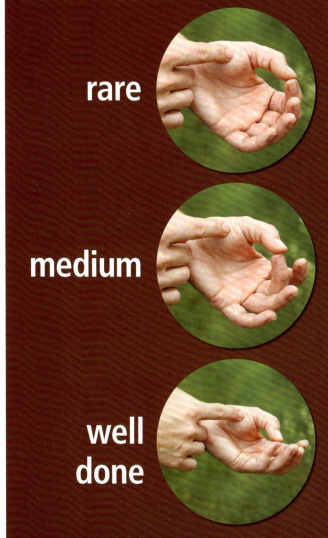

rare

medium

well done

ready or not?

Coals are ready for grilling when they are covered with gray ash, typically 25 to 30 minutes after you light them.

To check the temperature of the coals, use a built-in or separate flat grill thermometer. Or carefully place the palm of your hand above the grill at the cooking level and count the number of seconds you can hold it there. With your hand above the grill, say, "One, I love grilling; two, I love grilling …; " and so on. Then check the chart, below, to determine the grill's temperature. (Note: When you use indirect grilling, hot coals provide medium-hot heat, and medium-hot coals provide medium heat.)

Hand-Holding Time	Thermometer	Temperature	Visual
2 seconds	400°F to 450°F	Hot (high)	Coals glowing and lightly covered with gray ash
3 seconds	375°F to 400°F	Medium-High	
4 seconds	350°F to 375°F	Medium	Coals glowing through a layer of ash
5 seconds	325°F to 350°F	Medium-Low	
6 seconds	300°F to 325°F	Low	Coals burning down and covered with a thick layer of ash

lighting the coals

If you're a charcoal grill aficionado, your first step to a tantalizing cookout is lighting and preheating the coals properly. (If you own a gas grill, just follow the manufacturer's directions and stop reading here.)

1. To start your charcoal grill, mound briquettes on the charcoal grate. You can also put the coals in a metal chimney to consolidate them for more efficient and faster heating. You'll need approximately 30 briquettes per pound of meat or enough to cover an area about 3 inches larger than the diameter of the food you plan to cook.
2. Apply some type of starter to the cold coals. If you use an electric starter, place the starter under the coals and plug it in, following the manufacturer's directions. For a chemical starter, you can choose from instant-lighting briquettes, lighter fluid, fire-starter gels, or paraffin fire starters. A word of caution: If you use a chemical starter, do not apply more once you have tried to light the fire.
3. Light the coals with a long match. Leave the grill uncovered as it preheats.
4. Let the coals burn until they turn ash gray (by day) or glow red (by night). This usually takes 25 to 30 minutes.
5. Once the coals are ready, use tongs to spread them for either direct or indirect cooking (see "Fire Up!" page 6).

to cover or not to cover?

That's the burning question. With its lid closed, a grill is like an oven. It reflects heat and cooks the food from all sides, thereby reducing cooking time. With a charcoal grill, it is important to keep the vents open to feed oxygen to the fire. Open the vents more to increase the temperature or partially close them to reduce the temperature. While there are no hard and fast rules, the following guidelines cover the topic:

Cover the Grill…
…when you grill larger food items using indirect grilling so they cook evenly on all sides.
…to control flare-ups by reducing the supply of oxygen fueling the fire.
…when you smoke foods so the smoke infuses the food with flavor.

Uncover the Grill …
…to prevent overcooking when you direct-cook thinner, smaller foods with short cooking times.
…when you need to monitor foods that could burn, such as steaks with brushed-on sauces.

tame the flame

Controlling the temperature of your coals during grilling is key to tender, juicy results. Tame or increase the flame in these ways:

✱ Adjust the vents in the grill's bottom or sides. Close them to restrict airflow and dampen the heat. Open them to promote heat. Leave the vents in the grill cover open at all times during cooking or the fire will be smothered.

✱ On a gas grill, adjust the temperature with the turn of a dial.

✱ To lower the temperature of charcoal, spread out the hot coals and let them burn down for 5 to 10 minutes.

✱ To build a hotter charcoal fire, use more coals and don't let them burn down. If you want more heat from burning coals, gently tap them with long-handle tongs to shake off excess ash, then move the coals closer together.

✱ If you grill for a long period (more than 1 hour) and the grill starts losing heat, use tongs to replenish the coals, adding 8 to 10 coals every 30 to 45 minutes. If you use presoaked wood chips, add them whenever you add coals to the grill.

Take the guesswork out of deciding

when your food is ready to take off the grill. Turn to this easy-to-use chart as a guide to capture perfectly grilled food.

Cut	Thickness/Weight	Grill Temperature	Doneness	Direct-Grilling Time	Indirect-Grilling Time	
Flank steak	¾ inch–1 inch thick	medium	medium (160°F)	17–21 minutes	23–28 minutes	**beef**
Hamburgers	¾ inch thick	medium	well (170°F)	14–18 minutes	20–24 minutes	
Porterhouse steak	1 inch thick	medium	medium (160°F)	12–15 minutes	20–24 minutes	
Ribeye, sirloin, and T-bone steaks; tenderloin	1½ inches thick	medium	medium (160°F)	18–23 minutes	25–28 minutes	
Chop	1 inch thick	medium	medium rare (145°F) / medium (160°F)	12–14 minutes / 15–17 minutes	16–18 minutes / 18–20 minutes	**lamb**
Chop	1 inch thick	medium	medium (160°F)	12–15 minutes	19–23 minutes	**veal**
Whole fish (dressed)	½ lb.–1½ lb.	medium	flakes when tested with fork	6–9 minutes per 8 oz.	15–20 minutes per 8 oz.	**fish**
Fillets, steaks	½ inch–1 inch thick	medium	flakes when tested with fork	4–6 minutes per ½-inch thickness	7–9 minutes per ½-inch thickness	
Sea scallops	12–15 per pound	medium	opaque	5–8 minutes	11–14 minutes	
Shrimp	medium-size / large-size	medium / medium	opaque / opaque	5–8 minutes / 7–9 minutes	8–10 minutes / 9–11 minutes	
Broiler, fryer	1½ lb.–1¾ lb., halves / 12 oz.–14 oz., quarters	medium / medium	180°F / 180°F	40–50 minutes / 40–50 minutes	1–1¼ hours / 50–60 minutes	**poultry**
Boneless, skinless chicken breast	4 oz.–5 oz.	medium	170°F	12–15 minutes	15–18 minutes	
Chicken pieces	2½ lb.–3 lb. total	medium	180°F	35–40 minutes	50–60 minutes	
Turkey tenderloin	8 oz.–10 oz.	medium	170°F	16–20 minutes	25–30 minutes	
Bone-in chop	1¼–1½ inches thick	medium	160°F	16–20 minutes	35–40 minutes	**pork**
Boneless chop	1¼–1½ inches thick	medium	160°F	14–18 minutes	30–35 minutes	
Sausages, cooked		medium		3–7 minutes		
Tenderloin	¾ lb.–1 lb.	medium-high	155°F		30–35 minutes	

just for STARTERS

Hot Ribeye Bites, *recipe page 13*

calypso SHRIMP COCKTAIL

Sail right by old-fashioned shrimp cocktail. This breezy lime-and-mint rendition is jazzed up with cumin, cayenne pepper, and jalapeño pepper.

Prep: 25 minutes
Chill: 30 minutes
Grill: 5 minutes
Makes: 8 appetizer servings

- 8 ounces fresh or frozen medium shrimp
- 3 tablespoons olive oil
- 2 tablespoons snipped fresh mint
- ¼ teaspoon salt
- ⅛ to ¼ teaspoon cayenne pepper
- ⅛ teaspoon ground cumin
- ¼ cup lime juice
- 1 cup yellow and/or red cherry tomatoes, halved and/or quartered
- 2 tablespoons thinly sliced green onion
- 1 fresh jalapeño chile pepper, seeded and finely chopped*
- Dash salt
- 6 cups torn mixed salad greens
- 1 avocado, halved, seeded, peeled, and sliced (optional)

1 Thaw shrimp, if frozen. Peel and devein shrimp, leaving tails intact if desired. Rinse shrimp; pat dry with paper towels. In a medium bowl combine shrimp, 1 tablespoon of the oil, 1 tablespoon of the mint, the ¼ teaspoon salt, the cayenne pepper, and cumin. Cover and chill for 30 minutes.

2 Meanwhile, in a small bowl combine remaining 2 tablespoons oil, remaining 1 tablespoon mint, and the lime juice; set aside. In another medium bowl combine tomatoes, green onion, jalapeño chile pepper, and the dash salt; set aside.

3 Thread shrimp onto metal or wooden skewers,** leaving ¼-inch space between shrimp. Place skewers on the grill rack directly over medium heat; grill for 5 to 8 minutes or until shrimp turn opaque, turning once halfway through grilling. Remove shrimp from skewers.

4 Toss tomato mixture and greens together. Place in martini glasses or on salad plates. Top with shrimp. Drizzle with lime juice mixture. If desired, garnish with avocado slices.

Nutrition Facts per serving: 86 cal., 6 g total fat (1 g sat. fat), 43 mg chol., 143 mg sodium, 3 g carbo., 1 g fiber, 6 g pro.

***Note:** Use caution when handling hot chile peppers. Wear disposable gloves and/or wash hands thoroughly after preparation.

****Test Kitchen Tip:** If using wooden skewers, soak in warm water while shrimp chills. Drain before using.

hot RIBEYE BITES

Choose a mild variety of pickled pepper unless your guests really like to turn up the heat.

Prep: 15 minutes
Grill: 11 minutes
Makes: about 24 appetizers

- ¼ cup jalapeño pepper jelly
- 2 tablespoons Kansas City steak seasoning
- 2 boneless beef ribeye steaks, cut 1 inch thick (about 1¼ pounds) or 1 boneless beef top sirloin steak
- 24 pickled baby banana chile peppers, jalapeño chile peppers, other mild baby chile peppers, and/or cornichons*

1 For glaze, in a small saucepan stir together pepper jelly and steak seasoning. Cook and stir for 1 to 2 minutes over low heat or until jelly is melted. Set aside.

2 For a charcoal grill, grill the steaks on the grill rack of an uncovered grill directly over medium coals to desired doneness, turning steaks once halfway through grilling and brushing with glaze during the last 5 minutes. For ribeye steaks, allow 11 to 15 minutes for medium-rare (145°F) or 14 to 18 minutes for medium (160°F). Or for top sirloin, allow 14 to 18 minutes for medium-rare or 18 to 22 minutes for medium. (For a gas grill, preheat grill. Reduce heat to medium. Place steaks on grill rack over heat. Cover and grill as above.)

3 Cut steak into 1-inch cubes. Top each cube with a pickled pepper. Serve immediately.

Nutrition Facts per appetizer: 47 cal., 1 g total fat (1 g sat. fat), 11 mg chol., 179 mg sodium, 3 g carbo., 0 g fiber, 5 g pro.

*Note: Use caution when handling hot chile peppers. Wear disposable gloves and/or wash hands thoroughly after preparation.

smoky wings WITH DOUBLE DIPPERS

Serve with a purchased barbecue sauce or spicy ketchup and turn your double dippers into triple players.

Prep: 25 minutes
Marinate: 1 hour
Grill: 25 minutes
Makes: 20 servings

- 2 pounds chicken wings and/or wing drumettes
- Salt and pepper
- 1 tablespoon sugar
- 1 tablespoon finely shredded lime peel
- 1 teaspoon celery seeds
- 2 cups mesquite, hickory, or fruitwood chips
- Cooking oil
- Spicy Pesto Ranch Dipper*
- Black Pepper Blue Cheese Dipper**
- Assorted fresh vegetables (optional)

1 Cut off and discard wing tips from chicken wings, if desired. Sprinkle chicken wings with salt and pepper. Toss wings, sugar, lime peel, and celery seeds together in a large bowl. Cover and chill for 1 hour. Soak wood chips in enough water to cover. Cover and set aside for 1 hour; drain.

2 Prepare grill for indirect grilling; test for medium heat above the pan. Add some of the drained wood chips according to grill manufacturer's directions. Pour 1 inch of water into the drip pan.

3 Place chicken wings on a lightly oiled grill rack over the drip pan. Cover and grill for 25 to 30 minutes or until an instant-read thermometer inserted into thickest portion of a wing reads 180°F and juices run clear, adding more wood chips as necessary. Brush with cooking oil during the last 15 minutes of cooking. Serve with Spicy Pesto Ranch Dipper and Black Pepper Blue Cheese Dipper. Accompany wings with assorted fresh vegetables, such as baby carrots and celery sticks, if desired.

*Spicy Pesto Ranch Dipper: Stir together ¼ cup mayonnaise or salad dressing, 3 tablespoons purchased ranch salad dressing, 2 tablespoons purchased basil pesto, and ⅛ to ¼ teaspoon ground red pepper in a medium mixing bowl. Cover and chill until needed.

**Black Pepper Blue Cheese Dipper: Stir together ¼ cup mayonnaise or salad dressing, ¼ cup crumbled blue cheese, 3 tablespoons buttermilk, and ¼ to ½ teaspoon freshly ground black pepper in a medium mixing bowl. Cover and chill until needed.

Nutrition Facts per serving: 174 cal., 15 g total fat (3 g sat. fat), 50 mg chol., 146 mg sodium, 1 g carbo., 0 g fiber, 8 g pro.

dijon pork skewers WITH APPLE-APRICOT CHUTNEY

The crisp texture and lively flavor of tart apples, such as Granny Smith, make the Apple-Apricot Chutney a tangy-sweet partner for the cider-splashed pork.

Prep: 45 minutes
Grill: 6 minutes
Makes: 18 to 20 appetizer servings

- 3 tablespoons apple cider or apple juice
- 2 tablespoons Dijon-style mustard
- ½ teaspoon dried thyme, crushed
- 1¼ pounds boneless pork loin
- Apple-Apricot Chutney*

1 In a small bowl stir together apple cider, mustard, and thyme; set aside. Trim fat from pork. Cut pork across the grain into thin slices; cut slices into strips about 1 inch wide. Loosely thread 2 pork strips, accordion-style, onto each skewer.** Brush the mustard mixture on all sides of pork.

2 For a charcoal grill, place skewers on the grill rack directly over medium-hot coals. Grill, uncovered, for 6 to 8 minutes or until pork is cooked through, turning once. (For a gas grill, preheat grill. Reduce heat to medium-high. Place skewers on the grill rack over heat. Cover and grill as above.)

3 To serve, transfer skewers to a serving platter; serve with Apple-Apricot Chutney.

*Apple-Apricot Chutney: In a medium saucepan stir together ½ cup packed brown sugar; ¼ cup white wine vinegar; 1 small clove garlic, minced; ½ teaspoon grated fresh ginger; and ¼ teaspoon ground cinnamon. Stir in 2 cups peeled, cored, chopped tart cooking apples (about 2 medium); ½ cup snipped dried apricots; and ¼ cup chopped onion. Bring to boiling; reduce heat. Cover and simmer for 10 minutes. Uncover and boil gently about 15 minutes more or until only a small amount of liquid remains. Remove from heat. Cool slightly. To serve, transfer to a serving bowl. (Or to store, transfer to an air-tight container. Cover and refrigerate for up to 2 days. To serve, let stand at room temperature for 30 minutes.)

Nutrition Facts per serving: 84 cal., 1 g total fat (0 g sat. fat), 20 mg chol., 57 mg sodium, 11 g carbo., 1 g fiber, 7 g pro.

**Note: If using wooden skewers, soak them in water for 30 minutes. Drain skewers before using.

grilled BLACK BEAN AND SWEET POTATO QUESADILLAS

Turning over these loaded tortillas on a hot grill can be a bit tricky. For best results, use a wide metal spatula to get underneath the entire tortilla and carefully flip it over.

Prep: 25 minutes
Grill: 7 minutes
Makes: 8 (2-wedge) servings

- ½ cup chopped onion
- 2 cloves garlic, minced
- 1 tablespoon olive oil
- 1 15½-ounce can black beans, rinsed and drained
- 1 tablespoon freshly squeezed lime juice
- 1 teaspoon dried oregano, crushed
- 1 teaspoon ground cumin
- 4 10-inch flour tortillas
- 1½ cup mashed, cooked sweet potatoes*
- 1 cup shredded Monterey Jack cheese (4 ounces)
- 1½ cups tightly packed baby fresh spinach
- ½ to ¾ cup purchased tomato salsa, corn salsa, and/or guacamole

1 In a large skillet cook onion and garlic in hot oil until tender. Stir in black beans, lime juice, oregano, and cumin; heat through. Set aside.

2 Place 1 tortilla each on four large plates. Layer one-fourth of the sweet potatoes, 2 tablespoons of the cheese, one-fourth of the bean mixture, one-fourth of the spinach, and another 2 tablespoons cheese over half of each tortilla. Fold each tortilla over filling, pressing gently.

3 For a charcoal grill, slide quesadillas from plates onto the grill rack directly over low coals. Grill, uncovered, for 3 to 4 minutes or until cheese begins to melt; carefully turn. Grill second side for 4 to 5 minutes or until tortillas are crisp and filling is heated. (For a gas grill, preheat grill. Reduce heat to low. Place quesadillas on the grill rack over heat. Cover and grill as above.)

4 Using a pizza wheel, cut each quesadilla into 4 wedges. Serve warm with tomato salsa, corn salsa, and/or guacamole.

*For mashed sweet potatoes: Wash, peel, and cut off woody portions and ends of about 12 ounces sweet potatoes. Cut into quarters. Cook, covered, in enough boiling salted water to cover for 25 to 30 minutes or until tender. (Or place in a casserole with ½ cup water. Microwave, covered, on 100% power (high) for 8 to 10 minutes or until tender, stirring once.) Drain and mash with a potato masher.

Nutrition Facts per serving: 223 cal., 8 g total fat (3 g sat. fat), 13 mg chol., 484 mg sodium, 32 g carbo., 5 g fiber, 8 g pro.

cedar-planked BRIE WITH PEACH RELISH

When fresh peaches are not in their prime, opt for thawed and chopped frozen peach slices.

Prep: 25 minutes
Soak: 1 hour
Cook: 45 minutes
Cool: 1 hour
Grill: 13 minutes
Makes: 12 servings

- 1 15x7x½-inch cedar grill plank
- 1 pound peaches, peeled, seeded, and chopped (2½ cups)
- ¾ cup packed brown sugar
- ¾ cup cider vinegar
- ¼ cup golden raisins
- 2 tablespoons finely chopped red onion
- 2 tablespoons finely chopped pickled ginger
- 1 teaspoon chili powder
- ¼ teaspoon curry powder
- 1 tablespoon pickling spices
- 1 teaspoon mustard seeds
- 1 13- to 15-ounce round Brie cheese
- Grilled bread slices or assorted crackers

1 For at least 1 hour before grilling, soak plank in enough water to cover. Weight down plank to keep it submerged during soaking. Drain plank.

2 For peach relish, in a medium nonreactive saucepan combine peaches, brown sugar, vinegar, raisins, onion, ginger, chili powder, and curry powder. Place pickling spices and mustard seeds on a 6-inch square of 100%-cotton cheesecloth, bring up corners, and tie with clean 100%-cotton kitchen string (or place spices and seeds in a tea ball); add to mixture in saucepan. Bring peach mixture to boiling; reduce heat. Simmer, uncovered, stirring frequently, about 45 minutes or until thickened. Remove from heat and cool for 1 to 2 hours. Remove and discard spice bag.

3 For a charcoal grill, place the plank on the grill rack directly over medium coals until it begins to char and pop (about 3 to 5 minutes). Turn plank over. Place Brie on charred side of plank. Cover grill and cook for 10 to 12 minutes or until Brie softens and sides just begin to droop. (For a gas grill, preheat grill. Reduce heat to medium. Place plank on grill rack. Cover and grill as above.)

4 Serve Brie on plank with some of the peach relish spooned over top of cheese. Serve with grilled bread slices or crackers and remaining relish.

Nutrition Facts per serving: 188 cal., 8 g total fat (5 g sat. fat), 31 mg chol., 204 mg sodium, 21 g carbo., 1 g fiber, 7 g pro.

grilled yellow peppers
WITH HERB-CAPER SAUCE

Serve the sweet and smoky grilled peppers with an intriguing caper topper on sourdough bread strips.

Prep: 40 minutes
Grill: 10 minutes
Stand: 10 minutes
Makes: 8 appetizer servings

- 4 medium yellow sweet peppers
- 8 large ½-inch-thick slices whole wheat or white sourdough peasant bread
- 3 tablespoons olive oil
- 2 cloves garlic, halved
- Herb-Caper Sauce*
- Freshly cracked black pepper
- Fresh chive or garlic chive blossoms (optional)

1 Quarter sweet peppers lengthwise. Remove and discard seeds and membranes. Brush sweet peppers and bread slices with oil. For a charcoal grill, grill sweet peppers, cut sides up, on the grill rack of an uncovered grill directly over medium-hot coals about 10 minutes or until pepper skins are blistered and dark. (For a gas grill, preheat grill. Reduce heat to medium-high. Place peppers on the grill rack over heat. Cover and grill as above.) Remove sweet peppers from grill. Wrap sweet peppers tightly in foil; let stand for 10 to 15 minutes or until cool enough to handle.

2 Meanwhile, for a charcoal grill, place bread slices on the grill rack directly over medium-hot coals. Grill, uncovered, for 1 to 2 minutes or until golden, turning once halfway through grilling. (For a gas grill, preheat grill. Reduce heat to medium-high. Place bread slices on rack over heat. Grill as above.) Rub bread slices with garlic halves; set aside.

3 Unwrap sweet peppers when they are cooled. Using a paring knife, gently pull the skin off sweet peppers. Cut sweet peppers into 1-inch-wide strips. Cut bread into 1-inch-wide strips. Spoon Herb-Caper Sauce onto peppers. Season to taste with black pepper and serve with grilled bread strips. If desired, garnish with chive blossoms.

*Herb-Caper Sauce: In a small bowl combine ¼ cup olive oil; 4 anchovy fillets, drained and finely chopped; 2 tablespoons snipped fresh parsley; 2 tablespoons finely chopped shallots; 1 tablespoon capers, finely chopped; 1 teaspoon snipped fresh tarragon; 1 teaspoon snipped fresh oregano; 1 teaspoon snipped fresh thyme; and 1 clove garlic, minced. Stir in 1 teaspoon white wine vinegar and dash salt. Makes about ½ cup.

Nutrition Facts per serving: 200 cal., 13 g total fat (2 g sat. fat), 2 mg chol., 244 mg sodium, 17 g carbo., 3 g fiber, 5 g pro.

tomato-brie POTATO SKINS

A savvy cook never lets food go to waste. In this case, after you scoop out the potato flesh, mash it with a little milk, butter, and salt and serve potatoes alongside your favorite grilled meat.

Prep: 30 minutes
Grill: 25 minutes
Makes: 10 appetizer servings

- 5 4- to 6-ounce potatoes and/or sweet potatoes
- 1 tablespoon olive oil
- 1 clove garlic, minced
- ¼ teaspoon salt
- 1 4½-ounce round Brie cheese, cut into ½-inch pieces
- 1 cup cherry tomatoes, quartered
- ¼ cup walnuts, toasted and chopped
- ¼ cup snipped fresh Italian (flat-leaf) parsley
- ⅛ to ¼ teaspoon crushed red pepper

1 Scrub potatoes; cut each potato in half lengthwise. In a small bowl combine the oil, garlic, and salt. Brush cut surfaces of the potatoes with the oil mixture.

2 For a charcoal grill, place potatoes, cut sides down, on the grill rack directly over medium coals. Grill, uncovered, for 20 to 25 minutes or until tender, turning once halfway through grilling. (For a gas grill, preheat grill. Reduce heat to medium. Place potatoes, cut sides down, on the grill rack over heat. Cover and grill as above.)

3 Carefully scoop out the inside of each potato half, leaving a ½-inch-thick shell (reserve scooped-out potato flesh for another use). In a medium bowl combine Brie pieces, cherry tomatoes, walnuts, parsley, and crushed red pepper. Spoon mixture into potato shells. Return potato shells, cut sides up, to grill; grill for 5 to 7 minutes more or until cheese is softened and filling is heated through.

Nutrition Facts per serving: 111 cal., 7 g total fat (3 g sat. fat), 13 mg chol., 85 mg sodium, 9 g carbo., 1 g fiber, 4 g pro.

grilled cherry tomatoes
WITH GARLIC

If your oven is heated up, but your grill is not, bake these juicy bites at 350°F for 4 to 5 minutes or until they are heated through.

Prep: 20 minutes
Grill: 4 minutes
Makes: 12 appetizers

- 24 cherry tomatoes, 1 to 1½ inches in diameter
- 4 cloves garlic, cut into slivers
- 1 tablespoon olive oil
- 1 teaspoon snipped fresh rosemary or parsley
- 1 teaspoon sugar
- ¼ teaspoon salt, coarse sea salt, or kosher salt

1 Remove stems, if necessary, from tomatoes. Using the tip of a sharp knife, pierce tomatoes. Carefully insert a sliver of garlic into each one.

2 Place tomatoes in the center of an 18x12-inch piece of foil. Drizzle tomatoes with olive oil; sprinkle with rosemary, sugar, and salt. Bring together the two long sides of the foil and seal with a double fold. Fold remaining edges together to completely enclose tomatoes.

3 For a charcoal grill, place tomatoes on the grill rack directly over medium coals. Grill, uncovered, for 4 to 5 minutes or until heated through. (For gas grill, preheat grill. Reduce heat to medium. Place tomatoes on the grill rack over heat. Cover and grill as above.)

4 To serve, carefully open hot, steamy foil packet. Transfer tomatoes to serving plate or platter. Sprinkle with additional salt and serve immediately.

Nutrition Facts per 2-tomato serving: 55 cal., 3 g total fat (1 g sat. fat), 5 mg chol., 103 mg sodium, 5 g carbo., 1 g fiber, 2 g pro.

creamy APRICOT AND ONION DIP

To make the fruit wedges easier to turn on the grill, thread a few of them onto two side-by-side skewers, leaving space between each, before grilling.

Prep: 15 minutes
Grill: 14 minutes
Cool: 10 minutes
Makes: 12 (¼-cup) servings

- 4 apricots or 2 nectarines (about ¾ pound), pitted and each cut into 8 wedges
- 2 teaspoons olive oil
- ¾ teaspoon chili powder
- 1 large sweet onion, cut into ½-inch-thick slices
- ¾ cup dairy sour cream
- ⅓ cup mayonnaise
- ½ teaspoon salt
- ⅛ teaspoon ground coriander
- ⅛ teaspoon cayenne pepper
- Baguette slices
- 2 tablespoons snipped fresh chives (optional)

1 In a medium bowl toss apricot wedges with 1 teaspoon of the oil and the chili powder to coat. Brush the onion slices with the remaining 1 teaspoon oil.

2 For a charcoal grill, place apricot wedges on the grill rack directly over medium coals. Grill, uncovered, for 3 to 4 minutes per side or until well marked and tender but still holding their shape. Grill the onion slices, uncovered, for 7 to 8 minutes per side until they have grill marks and are tender. (For a gas grill, preheat grill. Reduce heat to medium. Place apricots and onions on the grill rack over heat. Cover and grill as above.) Transfer apricots and onion slices to a cutting board and cool for 10 minutes.

3 Meanwhile, in a medium bowl, combine the sour cream, mayonnaise, salt, coriander, and cayenne pepper. When the apricots and onion are cool, chop onions into small pieces and stir onion pieces into the sour cream mixture. Coarsely chop apricots and spoon on dip. Stir apricots into dip just before serving. Serve immediately or for more flavor refrigerate dip at least 1 hour. Serve with baguette slices sprinkled with chives.

Nutrition Facts per serving: 86 cal., 8 g total fat (3 g sat. fat), 7 mg chol., 138 mg sodium, 3 g carbo., 0 g fiber, 1 g pro.

brandied BLUE CHEESE BREAD

If you find a bottle of brandy in your cupboard, add a splash. If not, the bread will still possess a wonderful blue cheese flavor without it.

Prep: 15 minutes
Grill: 10 minutes
Makes: 12 servings

- 1 12- to 16-ounce baguette-style French bread
- ½ cup butter, softened
- ½ cup crumbled blue cheese (2 ounces)
- 1 tablespoon brandy (optional)
- 1 tablespoon snipped fresh chives
- ⅛ teaspoon cayenne pepper

1 Using a serrated knife, cut bread diagonally into 1-inch slices, cutting to but not through the bottom crust.

2 In a small bowl stir together butter, blue cheese, brandy (if using), chives, and cayenne pepper. Spread butter mixture between slices of bread. Wrap loaf tightly in heavy foil.

3 For a charcoal grill, place loaf on the grill rack directly over medium coals. Grill, uncovered, for 10 to 12 minutes or until bread is hot and cheese is melted, turning occasionally. (For a gas grill, preheat grill. Reduce heat to medium. Place loaf on the grill rack over heat. Cover and grill as above.)

Nutrition Facts per serving: 166 cal., 10 g total fat (6 g sat. fat), 24 mg chol., 305 mg sodium, 16 g carbo., 1 g fiber, 5 g pro.

eggplant DIP

Prep: 45 minutes
Grill: 13 minutes
Makes: about 20 (¼-cup) servings

- 2 bulbs garlic
- ½ cup extra virgin olive oil
- 2 1-pound eggplants, sliced ¾-inch thick
- 2 medium red sweet peppers, seeded and quartered lengthwise
- 1 teaspoon salt
- ⅓ cup lemon juice
- ¼ cup snipped fresh Italian (flat-leaf) parsley
- 2 tablespoons snipped fresh oregano
- Oregano leaves (optional)
- Purchased flatbreads, broken

1 Remove papery outer layers from garlic bulb. Cut off about ½ inch from top of bulb and discard. Place garlic in center of a 12-inch double-thick square of heavy foil. Bring foil up around garlic to form a cup. Drizzle garlic with 1 tablespoon of the olive oil. Twist ends of foil to completely enclose the garlic in foil.

2 Drizzle ¼ cup olive oil over eggplant slices and red sweet peppers and sprinkle with salt; toss to coat. For a charcoal grill, grill garlic packet on the grill rack directly over medium coals. Grill, uncovered, for 5 minutes. Add eggplant and pepper slices to grill. Grill for 8 to 10 minutes longer or until garlic cloves are soft when pressed, eggplant is tender, and peppers are tender and lightly charred, turning garlic packet, eggplant, and peppers once halfway through grilling time.

3 Coarsely chop eggplant and peppers. Transfer eggplant and peppers to a large glass or nonreactive bowl. Squeeze garlic pulp from individual cloves into a small bowl; use a potato masher or the back of a spoon to mash the pulp. Add remaining 3 tablespoons oil and lemon juice to garlic; whisk to combine. Add garlic mixture, parsley, and snipped oregano to eggplant mixture; toss to combine.

4 Serve immediately or let mixture stand, covered, up to 1 hour before serving. Or cover and chill mixture up to 3 days; let stand at room temperature 30 minutes before serving. Garnish with oregano leaves, if desired. Serve with flatbread pieces.

Nutrition Facts per serving: 111 cal., 6 g fat (1 g sat. fat), 0 mg chol., 199 mg sodium, 13 g carbo., 2 g fiber, 2 g pro.

cheesy GARLIC BREAD ON A STICK

Cubes of bread drizzled with garlic butter and tossed in Asiago cheese make a fun presentation when threaded on skewers and grilled to golden perfection.

Prep: 20 minutes
Grill: 5 minutes
Makes: 6 to 8 servings

- ¼ cup olive oil
- ¼ cup butter
- 3 cloves garlic, minced
- 1 16-ounce loaf baguette-style French bread
- ⅓ cup freshly grated Asiago cheese

1 In a small saucepan combine olive oil, butter, and garlic. Cook and stir over low heat until butter melts.

2 Using a serrated knife, cut bread into 1½-inch cubes. Place bread cubes in an extra-large bowl. Drizzle garlic mixture over bread cubes; toss to coat. Sprinkle with Asiago; toss to coat. Thread bread cubes on six to eight 10-inch skewers.*

3 For a charcoal grill, place skewers on the grill rack directly over medium coals. Grill, uncovered, for 5 to 10 minutes, turning often to brown evenly. (For a gas grill, preheat grill. Reduce heat to medium. Place skewers on the grill rack over heat. Cover and grill as above.) Serve immediately.

Nutrition Facts per serving: 392 cal., 20 g total fat (8 g sat. fat), 26 mg chol., 614 mg sodium, 43 g carbo., 2 g fiber, 13 g pro.

***Note:** If using wooden skewers, soak them in water for at least 30 minutes before grilling. Drain skewers before using.

cheddar-bacon LOAF

Besides being rich and buttery, this cheesy loaf gets a tangy boost from a smidgen of mustard.

Prep: 10 minutes
Grill: 10 minutes
Makes: 12 servings

- 1 16-ounce loaf baguette-style French bread
- ½ cup butter, softened
- 1 cup shredded sharp cheddar cheese (4 ounces)
- 6 slices bacon, crisp-cooked, drained, and crumbled
- ¼ cup sliced green onions (2)
- 2 teaspoons yellow mustard
- 1 teaspoon freshly squeezed lemon juice

1 Using a serrated knife, cut bread crosswise into 1-inch slices, cutting to but not through the bottom crust.

2 In a small bowl stir together butter, cheese, bacon, onions, mustard, and lemon juice. Spread mixture on both sides of bread slices. Wrap loaf tightly in heavy foil.

3 For a charcoal grill, place loaf on the grill rack directly over medium coals. Grill, uncovered, about 10 minutes or until cheese is melted and bread is heated through, turning once. (For a gas grill, preheat grill. Reduce heat to medium. Place loaf on the grill rack over heat. Cover and grill as above.)

Nutrition Facts per serving: 238 cal., 13 g total fat (8 g sat. fat), 35 mg chol., 461 mg sodium, 22 g carbo., 1 g fiber, 10 g pro.

walnut, onion, AND PROSCIUTTO BRUSCHETTA

Mild, sweet onions are at their best in spring and early summer—the perfect time to serve these crispy bruschetta. Look for Vidalia, Walla Walla, Maui, Texas Spring Sweet, Imperial Sweet, or Carzalia Sweet onions.

Prep: 25 minutes
Grill: 12 minutes
Makes: 8 bruschetta

Short wooden skewers or toothpicks

- 1 medium sweet onion, cut into ¾-inch slices
- 1 tablespoon olive oil
- ¼ cup walnuts, toasted and chopped
- 2 ounces prosciutto, chopped
- 3 tablespoons bottled balsamic vinaigrette
- 8 ½-inch slices crusty country bread
- ½ cup finely shredded smoked provolone or smoked Gouda cheese (2 ounces)
- 2 tablespoons snipped fresh oregano or 2 teaspoons snipped fresh thyme

1 To hold onion slices together during grilling, soak short wooden skewers in water for 20 minutes. Insert skewers into onion slices from the sides to the centers. Brush onion slices lightly with olive oil.

2 For a charcoal grill, grill onion slices on the rack of an uncovered grill directly over medium coals for 10 to 12 minutes or until tender, turning once halfway through grilling. Grill bread slices on grill rack directly over coals for 1 to 2 minutes or until toasted (do not turn). (For a gas grill, preheat grill. Reduce heat to medium. Place onion directly over heat. Cover and grill as above.) Remove onions from grill and place on cutting board; cool slightly. Remove and discard skewers. Coarsely chop onion.

3 In a small bowl combine walnuts and prosciutto. Add onion and balsamic vinaigrette, and toss to coat. Spoon mixture evenly onto toasted side of bread slices; sprinkle with cheese. Place slices on grill, topping side up. Cover and grill about 2 minutes or just until heated through and bottoms are toasted. Sprinkle with fresh oregano before serving.

Nutrition Facts per bruschetta: 214 cal., 10 g total fat (2 g sat. fat), 10 mg chol., 547 mg sodium, 24 g carbo., 1 g fiber, 8 g pro.

grilled parmesan BREADSTICKS

These buttery breadsticks disappear quickly. You might want to keep the ingredients for a second batch on hand.

Prep: 10 minutes
Grill: 2 minutes
Makes: 8 breadsticks

- ½ cup grated Parmesan cheese (2 ounces)
- 1¼ teaspoons dried Italian seasoning, crushed
- ¼ teaspoon crushed red pepper
- 8 purchased soft breadsticks
- 3 tablespoons butter, melted

1 In a shallow dish stir together the Parmesan cheese, Italian seasoning, and crushed red pepper; set aside. Brush breadsticks with butter. Roll each breadstick in the cheese mixture to coat.

2 For a charcoal grill, grill breadsticks on the rack of an uncovered grill directly over medium coals for 2 to 3 minutes or until golden, turning to brown evenly. (For a gas grill, preheat grill. Reduce heat to medium. Place breadsticks on grill rack over heat. Grill as above.) Serve warm.

Nutrition Facts per breadstick: 194 cal., 7 g total fat (4 g sat. fat), 16 mg chol., 430 mg sodium, 25 g carb., 1 g dietary fiber, 7 g protein.

Grilled Greek Breadsticks: Prepare as above, except use grated Romano cheese in place of the Parmesan, use Mediterranean seasoning in place of the Italian seasoning, omit the crushed red pepper, and add ½ teaspoon finely shredded lemon peel to the cheese mixture.

burgers, SANDWICHES, AND WRAPS

Chicken Sandwiches with Roasted Pepper-Goat Cheese Spread, *recipe page 66*

burgers WITH ONION JAM

Prepare the Onion Jam for the burgers a day or two in advance; cover and chill until needed.

Prep: 10 minutes
Grill: 18 minutes
Makes: 6 servings

- 2 pounds ground beef
- Onion Jam*
- 4 ounces goat cheese (chèvre)
- 1 teaspoon salt
- ½ teaspoon crushed red pepper
- 12 slices grilled Texas toast
- Goat cheese (chèvre) (optional)

1 In a large bowl combine ground beef, half of the Onion Jam, the goat cheese, salt, and crushed red pepper. Shape mixture into six 1-inch-thick patties.

2 For a charcoal grill, grill patties on the rack of an uncovered grill directly over medium coals for 18 to 23 minutes or until done (160°F), turning once halfway through grilling. (For a gas grill, preheat grill. Reduce heat to medium. Place patties on grill rack over heat. Cover and grill as above.)

3 Serve on Texas toast with Onion Jam and, if desired, additional goat cheese.

*Onion Jam: In a large skillet heat 2 tablespoons cooking oil over medium heat. Add 2 large yellow onions, thinly sliced, and 2 large red onions, thinly sliced; cook and stir for 5 minutes. Stir in 2 cups chopped green onions; cook for 25 to 30 minutes or until browned, stirring occasionally. Add ½ cup balsamic vinegar and ¼ cup packed brown sugar; reduce heat. Simmer for 10 to 12 minutes or until most of the liquid evaporates. Remove from heat. Cover and chill for up to 1 week.

Nutrition Facts per serving: 597 cal., 29 g total fat (11 g sat. fat), 104 mg chol., 1,047 mg sodium, 44 g carbo., 3 g fiber, 37 g pro.

grilled BURGERS ITALIANO

Two of America's favorites foods—hamburgers and pizza—come together in patties flavored with Italian staples.

Prep: 30 minutes
Grill: 10 minutes
Makes: 8 servings

- 1 egg, slightly beaten
- 1¼ cups meatless spaghetti sauce
- ½ cup fine dry bread crumbs
- ⅓ cup chopped onion
- 2 cloves garlic, minced
- 1 teaspoon dried basil or oregano, crushed
- 1 pound lean ground beef
- 1 pound bulk Italian sausage
- 2 medium green, yellow, and/or red sweet peppers, cut into rings and halved
- 1 tablespoon olive oil or cooking oil
- 1 6-ounce pkg. sliced mozzarella cheese, halved crosswise
- 8 kaiser rolls, split and toasted

1 In a large bowl combine egg and ¼ cup of the spaghetti sauce; stir in bread crumbs, onion, garlic, and basil. Add ground beef and sausage; mix well. Shape meat mixture into eight ½-inch-thick patties.

2 Fold a 24x18-inch piece of heavy foil in half to make an 18x12-inch rectangle. Place sweet peppers in center of foil; drizzle with oil. Bring up two opposite edges of foil and seal with a double fold. Fold remaining ends to completely enclose peppers, leaving space for steam to build.

3 Place patties and foil packet on the rack of an uncovered grill directly over medium coals. Grill for 10 to 13 minutes or until burgers are done (160°F) and peppers are tender, turning burgers and foil packet once halfway through grilling.

4 Top burgers with grilled sweet peppers and cheese. Cover and grill about 15 seconds more or until cheese is melted. Meanwhile, heat the remaining 1 cup spaghetti sauce.

5 Serve burgers in rolls topped with some of the spaghetti sauce. Pass the remaining sauce.

Nutrition Facts per serving: 540 cal., 27 g total fat (10 g sat. fat), 106 mg chol., 995 mg sodium, 41 g carbo., 0 g fiber, 31 g pro.

jerk burgers WITH MANGO SALSA

Prep: 20 minutes
Grill: 10 minutes
Makes: 4 servings

- 1 tablespoon cooking oil
- 1 cup finely chopped green sweet pepper
- ¼ cup finely chopped red sweet pepper
- ¼ cup finely chopped onion
- 1 teaspoon grated fresh ginger
- 1 medium mango, seeded, peeled, and chopped
- ¼ cup apple jelly
- 1 tablespoon lime juice
- Dash salt
- 1 egg, lightly beaten
- ⅓ cup bottled jerk sauce
- ¼ cup fine dry bread crumbs
- 1 pound lean ground beef
- 4 ciabatta rolls or hamburger buns, split
- 1 cup shredded Monterey Jack cheese (4 ounces)

1 For salsa, in a medium saucepan heat oil over medium heat. Add sweet peppers, onion, and ginger; cook and stir for 3 minutes. Add mango, jelly, lime juice, and salt; cook and stir until jelly is melted. Set aside.

2 In a large bowl combine egg, ¼ cup of the jerk sauce, and the bread crumbs. Add ground beef; mix well. Shape mixture into four ½-inch-thick patties.

3 For a charcoal grill, place patties on the rack of an uncovered grill directly over medium coals. Grill for 10 to 13 minutes or until done (160°F), turning and brushing once with the remaining jerk sauce halfway through grilling. If desired, toast ciabatta rolls on the grill. (For a gas grill, preheat grill. Reduce heat to medium. Place patties, then ciabatta rolls (if desired) on grill rack over heat. Cover and grill as above.)

4 Divide cheese among bottoms of rolls. Serve burgers in rolls with some of the salsa. Pass the remaining salsa.

Nutrition Facts per serving: 808 cal., 50 g total fat (20 g sat. fat), 167 mg chol., 740 mg sodium, 60 g carbo., 3 g fiber, 31 g pro.

backyard BURGERS

In the category of outdoor family meals, burgers head the list of grilling favorites. Dress them up in style with one or both of these tasty toppers.

Prep: 15 minutes
Grill: 14 minutes
Makes: 4 servings

- 1 slightly beaten egg white
- ½ cup soft bread crumbs
- ½ teaspoon salt
- ⅛ teaspoon black pepper
- 1 pound lean ground beef or ground veal
- 4 seeded hamburger buns, split
- 4 lettuce leaves
- Pesto Topper*
- Squished Tomato Topper**

1 In a large bowl combine egg white, bread crumbs, salt, and pepper. Add ground beef; mix well. Shape mixture into four ¾-inch-thick patties.

2 For a charcoal grill, grill patties on the rack of an uncovered grill directly over medium coals for 14 to 18 minutes or until done (160°F), turning once halfway through grilling. (For a gas grill, preheat grill. Reduce heat to medium. Place patties on grill rack over heat. Cover and grill as above.)

3 Serve burgers on buns with lettuce, Pesto Topper, and Squished Tomato Topper.

*Pesto Topper: In a small bowl stir together ¼ cup mayonnaise or salad dressing and 1 tablespoon purchased basil pesto.

**Squished Tomato Topper: Peel and seed 2 ripe tomatoes. In a medium bowl mash the tomatoes with a fork. Stir in 2 teaspoons olive oil and 2 teaspoons balsamic vinegar. Season to taste with salt and black pepper.

Nutrition Facts per serving: 526 cal., 32 g total fat (8 g sat. fat), 77 mg chol., 819 mg sodium, 29 g carbo., 2 g fiber, 28 g pro.

spiced pork burgers WITH MANGO MAYONNAISE

The versatile burger does it again: Try this one featuring ginger, curry powder, allspice, and a refreshing fruit-and-mayonnaise topping.

Prep: 25 minutes
Grill: 14 minutes
Makes: 6 servings

- 2 tablespoons dry white wine or water
- 2 tablespoons fine dry bread crumbs
- 1 to 2 tablespoons bottled hot pepper sauce
- 3 to 4 teaspoons grated fresh ginger
- 3 to 4 teaspoons curry powder
- ½ teaspoon salt
- ½ teaspoon ground allspice
- 4 cloves garlic, minced
- 1½ pounds ground pork
- 6 ¼-inch-thick slices sweet onion (such as Vidalia or Maui)
- 6 hamburger buns, split and toasted
- Lettuce leaves or 1 bunch stemmed watercress
- Mango Mayonnaise*

1 In a medium bowl combine wine, bread crumbs, hot pepper sauce, ginger, curry powder, salt, allspice, and garlic. Add ground pork; mix well. Shape pork mixture into six ¾-inch-thick patties.

2 For a charcoal grill, grill meat and onion slices on the grill rack of an uncovered grill for 14 to 18 minutes or until meat is done (160°F), turning once halfway through grilling. (For a gas grill, preheat grill. Reduce heat to medium. Place meat and onion slices on grill rack over heat. Cover and grill as above.)

3 Serve burgers on buns with grilled onion slices, lettuce, and Mango Mayonnaise.

***Mango Mayonnaise:** In a small bowl combine ½ cup finely chopped, peeled mango; ¼ cup mayonnaise or light mayonnaise dressing; and 2 teaspoons lime juice. Cover; chill for up to 24 hours.

Nutrition Facts per serving: 357 cal., 18 g total fat (5 g sat. fat), 60 mg chol., 578 mg sodium, 29 g carbo., 2 g fiber, 19 g pro.

gruyère AND PORK SANDWICHES

Prep: 15 minutes
Grill: 1 hour
Stand: 10 minutes
Makes: 8 servings

- 1 2-pound boneless pork top loin roast (single loin)
- 1 tablespoon paprika
- 1 teaspoon dried oregano, crushed
- ½ teaspoon salt
- ½ teaspoon garlic powder
- Coarse-grain brown mustard
- 1 10- to 12-inch Italian flat bread (focaccia), split horizontally and toasted
- 3 ounces thinly sliced cooked ham
- 4 slices Gruyère or Swiss cheese (about 4 ounces)
- Dill pickle slices

1 Trim fat from meat. For rub, in a small bowl combine paprika, oregano, salt, and garlic powder. Sprinkle rub evenly over meat; rub in with your fingers. Insert a meat thermometer into the center of meat.

2 For a charcoal grill, arrange medium coals around a drip pan. Test for medium-low heat above the pan. Cover and grill for 1 to 1¼ hours or until thermometer registers 155°F. For a gas grill, preheat grill. Reduce heat to medium-low. Adjust for indirect cooking. Grill as above, except place meat on a rack on a roasting pan. Remove meat from grill. Cover with foil; let stand for 10 minutes before carving. (The meat's temperature will rise 5°F during standing.)

3 To serve, thinly slice meat. Spread mustard on the bottom halves of bread. Layer with grilled pork, ham, cheese, and pickles. Spread mustard on top halves of bread; press firmly onto sandwiches. Cut into wedges.

Nutrition Facts per serving: 344 cal., 15 g total fat (6 g sat. fat), 72 mg chol., 425 mg sodium, 25 g carbo., 2 g fiber, 28 g pro.

glazed TURKEY BURGERS

A glaze of mustard and fruit preserves lends these burgers a sweet-sour dimension.

Prep: 20 minutes
Grill: 14 minutes
Makes: 4 servings

- 1 tablespoon yellow mustard
- 1 tablespoon cherry, apricot, peach, or pineapple preserves
- 1 beaten egg
- ¼ cup quick-cooking rolled oats
- ¼ cup finely chopped celery
- 3 tablespoons snipped dried tart cherries or dried apricots (optional)
- ¼ teaspoon salt
- ⅛ teaspoon black pepper
- 1 pound uncooked ground turkey or chicken
- 4 kaiser rolls or hamburger buns, split and toasted
- Mayonnaise or salad dressing, lettuce leaves, and/or tomato slices (optional)

1 For glaze, stir together mustard and preserves; set aside. In a medium bowl combine egg, rolled oats, celery, dried cherries (if desired), salt, and pepper. Add ground turkey; mix well. Shape turkey mixture into four ¾-inch-thick patties.

2 For a charcoal grill, grill patties on the rack of an uncovered grill directly over medium coals for 14 to 18 minutes or until no longer pink (170°F), turning once halfway through grilling and brushing with glaze during the last minute of grilling. (For a gas grill, preheat grill. Reduce heat to medium. Place burgers on grill rack over heat. Cover and grill as above.)

3 Serve burgers on buns. Brush any remaining glaze over burgers. If desired, serve burgers with mayonnaise, lettuce, and tomato.

Nutrition Facts per serving: 397 cal., 14 g total fat (3 g sat. fat), 143 mg chol., 599 mg sodium, 38 g carbo., 2 g fiber, 28 g pro.

fish burgers WITH DILLED SLAW

Prep: 30 minutes
Grill: 10 minutes
Makes: 6 servings

- 1½ pounds fresh or frozen tuna and/or salmon fillets
- ¼ cup snipped fresh cilantro
- 2 tablespoons lime juice
- 2 tablespoons olive oil
- 1 tablespoon pickled sushi ginger, finely chopped
- 1 tablespoon Asian chili sauce
- 1 to 2 teaspoons prepared wasabi paste
- 2 cloves garlic, minced
- ¼ teaspoon salt
- ¼ teaspoon ground black pepper
- 3 pita bread rounds, quartered
- Green Cabbage Slaw*
- Coarsely chopped tomato (optional)

1 Thaw fish, if frozen. Rinse fish; pat dry with paper towels. Finely chop fish.** In a large bowl combine fish, cilantro, lime juice, 4 teaspoons of the oil, the ginger, chili sauce, wasabi paste, garlic, salt, and pepper. Shape mixture into six ¾-inch-thick patties.

2 For a charcoal grill, place patties on the greased rack of an uncovered grill directly over medium coals. Grill for 10 to 12 minutes or until done (160°F), turning once halfway through grilling. Brush pita quarters with the remaining oil. Toast pita quarters on the grill. (For a gas grill, preheat grill. Reduce heat to medium. Place patties, then pita quarters on greased grill rack over heat. Cover and grill as above.)

3 Serve burgers between pita quarters with Green Cabbage Slaw and, if desired, chopped tomato.

*Green Cabbage Slaw: In a food processor or blender, combine ½ cup plain low-fat yogurt; 2 tablespoons snipped fresh parsley; 2 tablespoons snipped fresh dill; 1 tablespoon lime juice; 1 to 2 cloves garlic, minced; ⅛ teaspoon salt; and ⅛ teaspoon ground black pepper. Cover and process or blend until smooth. In a large bowl combine 3 cups finely shredded Napa cabbage and the yogurt mixture; toss gently to coat. Cover and chill for up to 24 hours.

Nutrition Facts per serving: 318 cal., 11 g total fat (2 g sat. fat), 44 mg chol., 408 mg sodium, 22 g carbo., 1 g fiber, 31 g pro.

**Tip: If you like, add the fish a little at a time into a food processor; cover and process with several on/off turns until finely chopped.

black bean BURGERS

Prep: 45 minutes
Grill: 37 minutes
Stand: 1 hour
Makes: 6 servings

- 1½ cups walnuts, toasted
- ⅔ cup chopped onion
- ⅔ cup snipped fresh cilantro
- 2 teaspoons ground cumin
- 3 cloves garlic
- ½ teaspoon dried oregano, crushed
- ½ teaspoon dried basil, crushed
- 2 15-ounce cans black beans, rinsed and drained
- ¼ cup canned diced green chile peppers, drained
- 2 eggs, lightly beaten
- ¾ cup fine dry bread crumbs
- ¼ teaspoon ground black pepper
- 2 fresh ears corn (with husks)
- 1 medium tomato, chopped
- ¼ cup finely chopped onion
- ¼ cup snipped fresh cilantro
- 1 teaspoon finely shredded lime peel
- 2 tablespoons lime juice
- 2 tablespoons olive oil
- ½ of a small fresh jalapeño chile pepper, seeded and finely chopped
- ¼ teaspoon salt
- ¼ teaspoon ground black pepper
- 6 English muffins, split

1 In a food processor fitted with a metal blade, combine walnuts, the ⅔ cup onion, the ⅔ cup cilantro, the cumin, garlic, oregano, and basil. Cover and process with several on-off turns just until combined. Add black beans and green chile peppers. Cover and process with several on-off turns just until combined. Transfer mixture to a large bowl. Stir in eggs, bread crumbs, and ¼ teaspoon black pepper. Using damp hands, shape mixture into six ¾-inch-thick patties. Place patties on a baking sheet, cover, and chill until ready to grill.

2 Carefully peel back corn husks, but do not remove. Using a stiff brush or your fingers, remove corn silks. Fold husks back around corn. Soak corn in enough water to cover for at least 1 hour.

3 While corn soaks, start preparing salsa. In a medium bowl combine tomato, the ¼ cup onion, the ¼ cup cilantro, the lime peel, lime juice, 1 tablespoon of the oil, the jalapeño pepper, salt, and ¼ teaspoon black pepper. Cover and chill until needed.

4 Drain corn; shake to remove excess water. Brush corn with the remaining 1 tablespoon oil. For a charcoal grill, place corn (with husks) on the rack of a grill with a cover directly over medium coals. Cover and grill for 25 to 30 minutes or until corn kernels are tender, turning corn several times. (For a gas grill, preheat grill. Reduce heat to medium. Place corn (with husks) on grill rack over heat. Cover and grill as above.) Carefully remove string and husks. Cut the corn kernels off cobs. Stir corn into salsa.

5 For charcoal grill, place patties on the grill rack directly over medium coals. Grill, uncovered, for 12 to 14 minutes or until done (160°F), turning once halfway through grilling. Toast English muffins on the grill. (For gas grill, place patties, then English muffins on grill rack over medium heat. Cover and grill as above.) Serve burgers between English muffin halves with salsa.

Nutrition Facts per serving: 595 cal., 28 g total fat (3 g sat. fat), 71 mg chol., 973 mg sodium, 70 g carbo., 12 g fiber, 22 g pro.

southwestern STEAK HERO

Herbed Crème Fraîche cools the heat generated by the peppery rub.

Prep: 20 minutes
Marinate: 4 to 8 hours
Grill: 14 minutes
Makes: 4 servings

- 1 1-pound boneless beef sirloin steak, cut 1 inch thick
- 3 tablespoons olive oil
- 1 tablespoon chili powder
- 1 tablespoon paprika
- 1 teaspoon ground cumin
- 1 teaspoon garlic powder
- 1 teaspoon dried oregano, crushed
- ½ teaspoon salt
- ½ teaspoon black pepper
- ½ teaspoon cayenne pepper
- 4 hoagie buns, split
- Sweet-hot mustard (optional)
- Cilantro Crème Fraîche*
- Prepared pico de gallo or bottled salsa (optional)

1 Trim fat from steak. For rub, in a small bowl combine oil, chili powder, paprika, cumin, garlic powder, oregano, salt, black pepper, and cayenne pepper. Sprinkle evenly over both sides of steak; rub in with your fingers. Place steak in a resealable plastic bag; close bag. Marinate in the refrigerator for 4 to 8 hours.

2 For a charcoal grill, grill steak on the rack of an uncovered grill directly over medium coals until desired doneness, turning once halfway through grilling. Allow 14 to 18 minutes for medium-rare (145°F) and 18 to 22 minutes for medium doneness (160°F). (For a gas grill, preheat grill. Reduce heat to medium. Place steak on the grill rack over heat. Cover and grill as above.) Remove steak from grill. Add buns, cut sides down, to grill. Grill for 1 to 2 minutes or until lightly toasted.

3 To serve, thinly slice steak. If desired, spread toasted buns with mustard. Top with steak slices, Cilantro Crème Fraîche, and if desired, pico de gallo.

*Cilantro Crème Fraîche: In a small bowl combine ½ of a 7-ounce container (about ½ cup) crème fraîche and 3 tablespoons snipped fresh cilantro.

Nutrition Facts per serving: 589 cal., 27 g total fat (8 g sat. fat), 91 mg chol., 882 mg sodium, 54 g carbo., 4 g fiber, 33 g pro.

blue cheese AND STEAK SANDWICHES

These hefty sandwiches make great picnic or tailgate fare. Prepare meat with rub, stir together spread, and clean or cut arugula and pepper at home. Then grill the steak and buns at the picnic and assemble.

Prep: 30 minutes
Chill: up to 2 days
Grill: 17 minutes
Stand: 10 minutes
Makes: 4 sandwiches

- 1 tablespoon packed brown sugar
- 2 teaspoons ground cumin
- 2 teaspoons garlic powder
- 1 teaspoon onion powder
- ½ teaspoon salt
- ¼ teaspoon ground black pepper
- 1 1¾-pound flank steak
- 4 sourdough or ciabatta buns, sliced and toasted
- ⅓ cup crumbled blue cheese
- ⅓ cup mayonnaise
- 1 teaspoon Worcestershire sauce
- 1 teaspoon white wine vinegar
- ½ cup fresh arugula
- ½ cup bottled roasted red sweet pepper

1 In a small bowl combine brown sugar, cumin, garlic powder, onion powder, salt, and pepper. Sprinkle mixture evenly over both sides of steak; rub in with your fingers. Wrap steak in plastic wrap and chill for up to 2 days.

2 For a charcoal grill, place steak on the grill rack directly over medium coals. Grill, uncovered, for 17 to 21 minutes or until an instant-read thermometer inserted in the center of steak registers 160°F, turning once halfway through grilling. (For a gas grill, preheat grill. Reduce heat to medium. Place steak on the grill rack over heat. Cover and grill as above.)

3 Transfer steak to a cutting board and let stand, loosely covered with aluminum foil, for 10 minutes. Thinly slice diagonally across the grain.

4 In a small bowl stir together blue cheese, mayonnaise, Worcestershire sauce, and vinegar. Spread the toasted side of bun bottoms with blue cheese mixture. Layer with sliced steak, arugula, and sweet pepper; add bun tops. Secure with wooden picks.

Nutrition Facts per sandwich: 684 cal., 29 g total fat (9 g sat. fat), 80 mg chol., 1,092 mg sodium, 48 g carbo., 1 g fiber, 53 g pro.

beef-spinach SANDWICHES

Prep: 20 minutes
Marinate: 4 to 24 hours
Grill: 17 to 21 minutes
Makes: 6 servings

- ¼ cup champagne vinegar or white wine vinegar
- 2 tablespoons Dijon-style mustard
- ¼ cup olive oil
- 2 teaspoons finely chopped shallots or sweet onion
- 1 teaspoon sugar
- ½ teaspoon salt
- ¼ teaspoon ground black pepper
- 1 1½-pound beef flank steak
- 6 hoagie buns, hamburger buns, or sourdough rolls, split
- 3 cups baby spinach
- 2 ounces goat cheese or feta cheese, crumbled
- ½ cup roasted red sweet pepper strips*

1 For marinade, stir together vinegar and mustard until mixture is smooth in a small bowl. Stir in olive oil, shallots, sugar, salt, and ground black pepper. Score both sides of steak in a diamond pattern by making shallow diagonal cuts at 1-inch intervals. Place steak in a resealable plastic bag set in a shallow dish. Pour marinade over steak; seal bag. Chill in refrigerator 4 to 24 hours, turning bag occasionally. Drain steak; discard marinade.

2 For a charcoal grill, grill steak on the rack of an uncovered grill directly over medium coals for 17 to 21 minutes for medium doneness (160°F), turning once. Add the hoagie buns to the grill rack, cut side down; grill about 1 minute or until toasted. (For a gas grill, preheat grill. Reduce heat to medium. Place steaks on grill rack. Cover and grill as above. Place buns on grill rack the last minute of grilling.)

3 Slice steaks across the grain into thin strips. Arrange spinach, steak, and cheese on bottom half of each grilled bun. Top with red pepper strips and bun tops.

*Roasted red pepper strips: Quarter a medium red sweet pepper. Remove stems, seeds, and membranes. Place pepper quarters, skin sides down, on grill rack directly over medium coals. Grill for 10 to 12 minutes or until skins are charred. Wrap peppers in foil and let stand 5 minutes. Use a sharp knife to loosen the skin edges; gently and slowly pull the skin from the pepper quarters. Discard skin. Cut pepper quarters into strips or ¾-inch pieces. (Or use purchased red sweet peppers; drain and cut into strips.)

Nutrition Facts per sandwich: 487 cal., 20 g fat (5 g sat. fat), 42 mg chol., 739 mg sodium, 51 g carbo., 2 g fiber, 26 g pro.

greek-inspired LAMB POCKETS

Be a dinnertime hero with a meal-in-a-pocket that will win you applause. Meaty lamb leg or shoulder is marinated in balsamic vinegar, pepper, and fresh herbs, quick-grilled to keep it juicy, then tucked into pitas and topped with a creamy yogurt sauce.

Prep: 20 minutes
Marinate: 10 minutes to 4 hours
Grill: 10 minutes
Makes: 4 servings

- 1 pound boneless lamb leg or shoulder
- ¼ cup balsamic vinegar
- 1 tablespoon snipped fresh savory or 1 teaspoon dried savory, crushed
- ½ teaspoon ground black pepper
- 1 8-ounce carton plain low-fat or fat-free yogurt
- 1 small cucumber, peeled, seeded, and chopped (¾ cup)
- 2 plum tomatoes, chopped
- 1 small onion, finely chopped
- 4 whole wheat pita bread rounds

1 Trim fat from lamb. Cut lamb into ½-inch thin strips. Place lamb in a resealable plastic bag set in a shallow dish. For marinade, in a small bowl combine vinegar, savory, and pepper. Pour marinade over lamb. Seal bag; turn once to coat meat. Marinate in the refrigerator for at least 10 minutes or up to 4 hours, turning bag occasionally.

2 Meanwhile, for sauce, in a medium bowl combine yogurt, cucumber, tomatoes, and onion. Cover and refrigerate until ready to serve or up to 4 hours. Wrap pita rounds in foil. Set aside.

3 Drain lamb, reserving marinade. On long metal skewers, thread lamb (accordion-style). For a charcoal grill, grill skewers on the rack of an uncovered grill directly over medium coals for 10 to 12 minutes or until done, turning once halfway through grill and brushing with reserved marinade for the first 5 minutes of grilling. Place the pita rounds on grill rack next to the kabobs for the last 5 minutes of grilling. (For a gas grill, preheat grill. Reduce heat to medium. Place kabobs on grill rack over heat. Cover and grill as above.) Discard any remaining marinade.

4 Cut pita bread rounds in half crosswise. Spoon the sauce into pita halves and fill with lamb strips.

Nutrition Facts per serving: 361 cal., 8 g total fat (3 g sat. fat), 61 mg chol., 430 mg sodium, 46 g carbo., 1 g fiber, 28 g pro.

grilled ITALIAN PANINI

You can find a capocollo (an Italian ham coated with peppery spices) at Italian delis and in some supermarkets. Substitute prosciutto or cured deli ham if capocollo isn't available.

Prep: 20 minutes
Grill: 8 minutes
Makes: 4 servings

- 1 16-ounce loaf unsliced ciabatta or Italian bread
- 6 ounces thinly sliced provolone cheese
- ¼ cup mayonnaise or salad dressing
- 1 tablespoon purchased basil pesto
- 4 ounces thinly sliced capocollo or cooked ham
- 4 ounces thinly sliced salami
- Red Onion Relish*
- 1 cup arugula
- 1 tablespoon olive oil

1 Carefully trim off and discard the top crust of the bread to make a flat surface. Turn bread over; trim off and discard bottom crust. Cut remaining bread in half horizontally to form two ½-inch slices.

2 Place half of the provolone cheese on 1 slice of bread. Combine mayonnaise and pesto in a small bowl; spread over cheese. Top with capocollo, salami, Red Onion Relish, arugula, remaining cheese, and the other slice of bread. Brush both sides of panini with oil.

3 For a charcoal grill, place on the lightly greased grill rack of an uncovered grill directly over medium coals. Put a 13x9x2-inch baking pan on top of sandwich; weigh down pan with several baking potatoes or a brick. Grill 5 minutes or until sandwich is lightly browned. Use hot pads to remove baking pan. Use a spatula to carefully turn over sandwich. Place baking pan back on sandwich; grill about 3 minutes more or until cheese melts. (For a gas grill, preheat grill. Reduce heat to medium. Place sandwich on grill rack over heat. Place pan on sandwich and grill as above.)

*Red Onion Relish: Combine 1 medium red onion, halved and thinly sliced (1 cup); 2 tablespoons olive oil; 1 tablespoon red wine vinegar; and 1 teaspoon snipped fresh oregano in a small bowl. Sprinkle with salt and ground black pepper as desired. Cover; let stand at room temperature for up to 2 hours.

Nutrition Facts per serving: 840 cal., 51 g total fat (15 g sat. fat), 77 mg chol., 2118 mg sodium, 62 g carbo., 4 g fiber, 33 g pro.

bratwurst WITH KICKIN' CRANBERRY KETCHUP

To keep it quick and easy, rely on your supermarkets deli for the coleslaw in this recipe.

Prep: 20 minutes
Grill: 3 minutes
Makes: 6 servings

- 6 cooked, smoked bratwurst
- 6 hoagie buns, split and toasted
- Kickin' Cranberry Ketchup*
- 1 cup prepared vinaigrette-style coleslaw

1 For a charcoal grill, grill bratwurst on the rack of an uncovered grill directly over medium coals for 3 to 7 minutes or until bratwurst are browned and heated through, turning once halfway through grilling. (For a gas grill, preheat grill. Reduce heat to medium. Place bratwurst on grill rack over heat. Cover and grill as above.)

2 Serve bratwurst in toasted buns; top with Kickin' Cranberry Ketchup and coleslaw.

*Kickin' Cranberry Ketchup: Coarsely chop ¼ cup dried cranberries; place in a small bowl. Add enough boiling water to cover; let stand 5 minutes. Drain cranberries. Stir in ⅓ cup catsup, 2 teaspoons prepared horseradish, and several dashes bottled hot pepper sauce.

Nutrition Facts per serving: 705 cal., 33 g total fat (10 g sat. fat), 52 mg chol., 1550 mg sodium, 84 g carbo., 5 g fiber, 21 g pro.

grilled brats WITH BLACK BEAN SALSA

The classic German sausage gets some Mexican flair. Dress up your brat with salsa or serve the salsa on the side with tortilla chips.

Prep: 15 minutes
Cook: 20 minutes
Grill: 20 to 25 minutes
Makes: 10 servings

- 10 uncooked bratwursts (about 4 ounces each)
- 2 medium onions, halved and thinly sliced (1 cup)
- 1 tablespoon cooking oil
- 2 14-ounce cans chicken broth
- 1 12-ounce can beer
- 10 hoagie buns, split and toasted
- Black Bean Salsa*

1 Pierce bratwursts in several places with tines of fork. For a charcoal grill, arrange preheated coals around a drip pan. Test for medium heat above pan. Place brats on rack over pan. Cover; grill bratwursts for 20 to 25 minutes or until juices run clear, turning occasionally. (For a gas grill, preheat grill. Reduce heat to medium. Adjust for indirect grilling. Place brats on grill rack. Cover and grill as above.)

2 Meanwhile, cook onions in hot oil in a Dutch oven until tender. Stir in broth and beer. Bring to boiling; reduce heat. Simmer, uncovered, for 20 minutes. Add cooked bratwursts; heat through.

3 Serve bratwursts on buns with onions. Top with Black Bean Salsa.

*Black Bean Salsa: In a medium bowl combine one 15-ounce can black beans, rinsed and drained; 1 medium cucumber, peeled, seeded, and chopped; 1 medium tomato, seeded and chopped; ½ cup sliced green onions; ¼ cup lime juice; 1 tablespoon snipped fresh cilantro; 1 tablespoon olive oil; ½ teaspoon ground cumin; ⅛ teaspoon salt; and ⅛ teaspoon cayenne pepper. Cover and chill for 4 to 24 hours.

Nutrition Facts per serving: 430 cal., 35 g total fat (17 g sat. fat), 68 mg chol., 1421 mg sodium, 9 g carbo., 3 g fiber, 15 g pro.

lemon-and-dill FISH SANDWICHES WITH TARTAR SAUCE

Grill the fish on a bed of lemon slices to infuse it with fresh citrus flavor and keep it deliciously moist.

Prep: 1 hour
Grill: 10 minutes
Makes: 6 sandwiches

- 24 to 36 ounces fresh or frozen skinless, boneless walleye pike, haddock, sole, tilapia or cod fillets, ¾ inch thick
- Salt
- Freshly ground black pepper
- 2 teaspoons finely shredded lemon peel
- 3 tablespoons lemon juice
- 3 tablespoons olive oil
- 2 tablespoons snipped fresh dill or 1 teaspoon dried dillweed
- 4 cloves garlic, minced
- ¼ to ½ teaspoon bottled hot pepper sauce
- 4 large lemons, cut into ¼-inch slices
- 12 slices country wheat bread, lightly buttered; or 6 hoagie buns, French-style rolls, or other crusty rolls, split and lightly buttered
- 3 cups packaged shredded cabbage with carrot (coleslaw mix) or packaged mixed salad greens
- 6 tomato slices
- Tartar Sauce*

1 Thaw fish, if frozen. Rinse fish; pat dry with paper towels. Sprinkle both sides of each fish fillet with salt and black pepper.

2 In a small bowl combine lemon peel, lemon juice, oil, dill, garlic, and hot pepper sauce.

3 Grease the unheated grill rack. For a charcoal grill, arrange a bed of lemon slices on the greased grill rack directly over medium coals. Arrange fish on lemon slices. Brush with the lemon-oil mixture. Grill, covered, for 10 to 12 minutes or until fish flakes easily when tested with a fork (do not turn fish). (For a gas grill, preheat grill. Reduce heat to medium. Arrange lemon slices and fish on greased grill rack over heat (line grill rack with foil if grids are too wide). Brush fish with lemon-oil mixture. Grill, covered, as above.) Place bread, cut sides down, next to fish the last 2 minutes of grilling or until toasted, turning bread slices once.

4 To serve, using a large spatula transfer fish pieces to 6 bread slices topped with shredded cabbage mix and tomato slices. Top with Tartar Sauce and remaining bread. Discard lemon slices.

***Tartar Sauce:** In a medium bowl stir together 1 cup mayonnaise or salad dressing, 2 tablespoons finely chopped sweet or dill pickle, 1 tablespoon finely chopped green onion or red onion, 1 tablespoon snipped fresh parsley, ½ teaspoon finely shredded lemon peel, 2 teaspoons lemon juice, 1½ teaspoons snipped fresh dill or ½ teaspoon dried dillweed, and ½ teaspoon paprika. Store any remaining Tartar Sauce in the refrigerator for up to 1 week.

Nutrition Facts per sandwich: 586 cal., 39 g total fat (7 g sat. fat), 111 mg chol., 642 mg sodium, 29 g carbo., 3 g fiber, 28 g pro.

shrimp po' boy WITH DRIED TOMATO AIOLI

Whether you call them heroes, grinders, hoagies, subs, or po' boys, these sandwiches are a step above the rest. Grilled shrimp and lettuce are loaded onto French bread and topped with a dried tomato mayo. Delicious by any name!

Prep: 30 minutes
Marinate: 1 hour
Grill: 7 minutes plus 12 minutes
Makes: 4 servings

- 1 pound fresh or frozen jumbo shrimp in shells
- 2 tablespoons lemon juice
- 2 tablespoons olive oil
- 1 teaspoon seafood seasoning (such as Old Bay)
- 1 8-ounce loaf or ½ of a 16-ounce loaf unsliced French bread
- ½ cup mayonnaise
- ¼ cup chopped dried tomatoes (oil-pack), drained
- 2 tablespoons dairy sour cream
- 2 cloves garlic, minced
- ½ of a medium red onion, thinly sliced
- Shredded lettuce (optional)

1 Thaw shrimp, if frozen. Peel and devein shrimp, removing tails. Rinse shrimp; pat dry with paper towels. Set aside. Place shrimp in a resealable plastic bag set in a shallow dish. In a small bowl stir together 1 tablespoon of the lemon juice, 1 tablespoon of the olive oil, and the seafood seasoning. Pour marinade over shrimp; seal bag. Marinate in the refrigerator for 1 hour, turning bag occasionally. Thread shrimp on four long metal skewers, leaving a ¼-inch space between pieces.

2 Halve bread horizontally. Use a spoon to hollow out the top half, leaving a ½-inch-thick shell. Lightly brush cut bread surface with remaining 1 tablespoon olive oil. For a charcoal grill, grill shrimp on a grill rack directly over medium coals for 7 to 9 minutes or until shrimp are opaque. Meanwhile add bread to grill. Grill about 2 minutes or until bread is lightly toasted. Remove bread from grill. (For a gas grill, preheat grill. Reduce heat to medium. Place shrimp and bread on grill rack over heat. Cover and grill as above.)

3 Meanwhile, in a small bowl stir together remaining 1 tablespoon lemon juice, the mayonnaise, dried tomatoes, sour cream, and garlic. Spread on cut surfaces of toasted bread. Place bottom spread side up in the center of an 18-inch square of heavy-duty foil. Arrange shrimp and red onion slices on bread bottom; add bread top. Bring up two opposite edges of foil and seal with a double fold. Fold remaining edges together to completely enclose. Return to grill; grill for 12 to 15 minutes or until heated through, turning once.

4 To serve, remove foil from po' boy. Remove top and, if desired, add lettuce. Replace top; cut into four equal pieces.

Nutrition Facts per serving: 542 cal., 34 g total fat (5 g sat. fat), 151 mg chol., 829 mg sodium, 34 g carbo., 2 g fiber, 23 g pro.

ham steak sandwiches
WITH APRICOT-CHERRY CHUTNEY

Lose the bun, if you like, and simply serve the sweet chutney over grilled ham steak.

Prep: 15 minutes
Cook: 10 minutes
Grill: 14 minutes
Stand: 15 minutes
Makes: 8 to 10 servings

- 1 cup dried apricots, coarsely snipped
- 1 cup dried cherries
- ½ cup golden raisins
- ¾ cup apricot preserves
- ⅓ cup thinly sliced green onions
- ¼ cup white wine vinegar
- 2 cloves garlic, minced
- 1 2-pound cooked center-cut ham slice, cut ½ inch thick
- 8 to 10 large potato rolls or hamburger buns, split and toasted
- 8 ounces thinly sliced havarti cheese

1 For chutney, in a medium bowl stir together apricots, cherries, and raisins. Add enough boiling water to cover; let stand 15 minutes. Drain. In a medium saucepan stir together drained fruit, apricot preserves, green onions, vinegar, and garlic. Bring to boiling; reduce heat. Simmer, uncovered, for 10 to 15 minutes or until thickened. Set chutney aside.

2 Trim fat from ham. For a charcoal grill, grill ham on the rack of an uncovered grill directly over medium coals for 14 to 18 minutes or until heated through (140°F). (For a gas grill, preheat grill. Reduce heat to medium. Place ham on grill rack over heat. Cover and grill as above.)

3 To serve, thinly slice ham. Serve on toasted rolls topped with cheese and chutney.

Nutrition Facts per serving: 672 cal., 26 g total fat (4 g sat. fat), 100 mg chol., 1,956 mg sodium, 77 g carbo., 4 g fiber, 33 g pro.

chicken sandwiches WITH ROASTED PEPPER-GOAT CHEESE SPREAD

Prep: 30 minutes
Marinate: 1 to 2 hours
Grill: 11 minutes
Makes: 4 servings

- 4 skinless, boneless chicken breast halves
- ¼ cup balsamic vinegar
- 2 tablespoons olive oil
- 1 tablespoon snipped fresh rosemary
- 2 cloves garlic, minced
- Salt and black pepper
- 1 10- to 12-inch rosemary or garlic Italian flat bread (focaccia)
- Roasted Pepper-Goat Cheese Spread*
- ½ of a medium red onion, thinly sliced
- 1 cup baby spinach leaves or small romaine leaves

1 Place a chicken breast half between two pieces of plastic wrap. Using the flat side of a meat mallet, pound the chicken lightly to about ½-inch thickness. Remove plastic wrap. Repeat with remaining chicken pieces.

2 Place chicken in a resealable plastic bag set in a shallow dish. For marinade, combine vinegar, oil, rosemary, and garlic. Pour over chicken; seal bag. Marinate in the refrigerator for 1 to 2 hours, turning bag occasionally.

3 Drain chicken, discarding marinade. Sprinkle lightly with salt and pepper. For a charcoal grill, grill chicken on the rack of an uncovered grill directly over medium coals for 9 to 11 minutes or until chicken is no longer pink (170°F), turning once halfway through grilling. (For a gas grill, preheat grill. Reduce heat to medium. Place chicken on grill rack over heat. Cover and grill as above.)

4 To serve, cut flat bread into 4 wedges. Slice each wedge in half horizontally. Grill cut side down directly over medium heat about 2 minutes or until lightly toasted. Spread toasted sides of bread with Roasted Pepper-Goat Cheese Spread. If necessary, cut chicken breasts to fit bread. Divide chicken, onions, and spinach among bread wedges. Add top bread wedges.

*Roasted Pepper-Goat Cheese Spread: Drain ¼ cup roasted red sweet peppers, reserving 1 teaspoon liquid. In a food processor bowl combine sweet peppers, reserved liquid, 4 ounces soft goat cheese (chèvre), and 1 teaspoon snipped fresh rosemary. Cover and process until nearly smooth. (Or finely chop the sweet pepper and stir mixture together with a wooden spoon.)

Nutrition Facts per serving: 321 cal., 12 g total fat (5 g sat. fat), 96 mg chol., 392 mg sodium, 11 g carbo., 1 g fiber, 40 g pro.

chicken SAUSAGE SANDWICHES

Piercing the sausage skins keeps the links from splitting as they sizzle on the grill.

Start to Finish: 30 minutes
Makes: 6 servings

- 1 medium sweet onion, halved and sliced (½ cup)
- 4 cloves garlic, minced
- 2 tablespoons olive oil
- 1 large yellow summer squash, halved lengthwise and thinly sliced (about 2 cups)
- 1 cup sliced mushrooms
- 2 tablespoons balsamic vinegar
- 2 teaspoons snipped fresh rosemary or ½ teaspoon dried rosemary, crushed
- ½ cup quartered cherry tomatoes
- 6 cooked chicken sausage links or cooked smoked sausage links
- 6 hoagie buns
- ½ cup shredded fresh spinach

1 In a large skillet cook onion and garlic in hot oil over medium-high heat for 3 minutes. Stir in squash and mushrooms. Cook and stir for 4 to 5 minutes more or until vegetables are tender. Stir in vinegar and rosemary. Remove from heat. Stir in quartered cherry tomatoes.

2 Meanwhile, pierce skin of sausages several times with a fork. For a charcoal grill, grill sausages on the rack of an uncovered grill directly over medium coals about 7 minutes or until sausages are browned and heated through, turning once halfway through grilling. (For a gas grill, preheat grill. Reduce heat to medium. Place sausages on grill rack over heat. Cover and grill as above.)

3 Halve the buns lengthwise, cutting to but not through the other side. Toast cut sides of buns alongside the sausages. Serve sausages in buns with onion mixture. Sprinkle with spinach.

Nutrition Facts per serving: 466 cal., 19 g total fat (5 g sat. fat), 20 mg chol., 1,007 mg sodium, 55 g carbo., 4 g fiber, 20 g pro.

chicken MOLE SANDWICH

It's the mole that makes this sandwich a zinger. Would you believe a sauce of chocolate and Mexican chile peppers could taste this good?

Prep: 25 minutes
Chill: 30 minutes
Grill: 12 minutes
Makes: 4 servings

- ¼ cup chopped onion
- 3 cloves garlic, minced
- 1 tablespoon cooking oil
- ½ cup water
- 3 dried chile peppers (New Mexico or pasilla), seeded and coarsely chopped
- 3 tablespoons chopped Mexican-style sweet chocolate or semisweet chocolate (1½ ounces)
- 4 medium skinless, boneless chicken breast halves (about 1 pound total)
- Salt (optional)
- 1 small avocado, seeded, peeled, and mashed
- 2 tablespoons light mayonnaise dressing
- ¼ teaspoon ground red pepper (optional)
- ⅛ teaspoon salt
- 4 hard rolls (about 6 inches in diameter), split and toasted
- Tomato slices
- Baby romaine or other lettuce leaves

1 For mole, in a large skillet cook onion and garlic in hot oil over medium-high heat until onion is tender. Add water and dried chile peppers. Reduce heat to medium; stir in chocolate. Cook and stir for 3 to 5 minutes or until thickened and bubbly. Cool slightly. Transfer mixture to a food processor bowl or blender container. Cover and process or blend until a smooth paste forms. Reserve 1 to 2 tablespoons of the mole.

2 If desired, sprinkle chicken with salt. Using a sharp knife, cut a slit horizontally two-thirds of the way through each chicken piece. Spread meat open; fill with remaining mole. Fold closed. Rub the outside of the chicken with the reserved mole.

3 For a charcoal grill, grill chicken on the rack of an uncovered grill directly over medium coals for 12 to 15 minutes or until tender and no longer pink, turning once halfway through. (For a gas grill, preheat grill. Reduce heat to medium. Place chicken on grill rack over heat. Cover and grill as above.) Cover and chill for 30 minutes.

4 In a small bowl stir together avocado, mayonnaise dressing, ground red pepper (if desired), and the ⅛ teaspoon salt. To serve, cut chicken into ¼- to ½-inch slices. Spread avocado mixture on split rolls; layer with tomato, chicken, and romaine.

Nutrition Facts per serving: 496 cal., 22 g total fat (5 g sat. fat), 59 mg chol., 542 mg sodium, 45 g carbo., 5 g fiber, 30 g pro.

salmon wraps WITH JICAMA SLAW

These tidy salmon and slaw wraps are great outdoor fare: No forks or knives necessary.

Prep: 25 minutes
Marinate: 30 minutes to 1 hour
Grill: 8 minutes
Makes: 4 servings

- 1 cup jicama cut into matchstick-size pieces
- 1 cup shredded cabbage
- 1 small tomato, seeded and chopped (⅓ cup)
- 2 tablespoons thinly sliced green onion (1)
- 1 tablespoon snipped fresh cilantro
- 1 to 2 serrano chile peppers, seeded and finely chopped
- ¼ cup apple juice
- 1½ teaspoons finely shredded lime peel
- 2 tablespoons lime juice
- 1 tablespoon salad oil
- ⅛ teaspoon salt
- ¼ teaspoon salt
- ¼ teaspoon pepper
- ¼ teaspoon dried oregano, crushed
- 1 1-pound skinless salmon fillet
- 4 10-inch flour tortillas
- 1 tablespoon salad oil

1 For slaw, in a large bowl combine jicama, cabbage, tomato, green onion, cilantro, and serrano pepper. In a small bowl combine apple juice, ½ teaspoon of the lime peel, the lime juice, 1 tablespoon oil, and the ⅛ teaspoon salt. Add to the jicama mixture; toss to combine. Cover and marinate in the refrigerator for 30 minutes to 1 hour, stirring once or twice.

2 Combine the remaining 1 teaspoon lime peel, the ¼ teaspoon salt, pepper, and oregano. Sprinkle over surface of salmon fillet; rub in. Lightly grease the grill rack.

3 Lightly grease or coat with nonstick cooking spray an unheated grill rack. For a charcoal grill, grill fish on the greased grill rack of an uncovered grill directly over medium coals for 8 to 12 minutes or until fish flakes easily when tested with a fork, turning once halfway through grilling. (For a gas grill, preheat grill. Reduce heat to medium. Place fish on greased grill rack over heat. Cover and grill as above.)

4 To serve, break salmon into pieces. Place one-fourth of the salmon just below the center of each tortilla. Using a slotted spoon, top each salmon portion with one-fourth of the slaw. Fold bottom edge of tortilla up over filling. Fold opposite sides in; roll up from the bottom. Secure with a wooden toothpick, if necessary. Brush filled tortillas lightly with remaining oil; place on grill rack directly over medium heat. Grill 3 to 4 minutes or until heated through, turning once. Cut in half to serve.

Nutrition Facts per serving: 419 cal., 21 g total fat (4 g sat. fat), 70 mg chol., 457 mg sodium, 31 g carbo., 2 g fiber, 28 g pro.

pork wraps WITH CORN-TOMATO RELISH

When you expect an evening with a dinner-hour dash, grill the pork and stir together the relish the night before. These wraps taste just as delicious served chilled.

Prep: 50 minutes
Grill: 30 minutes
Stand: 15 minutes
Makes: 10 wraps

- 2 1-pound pork tenderloins
- Salt
- Freshly ground black pepper
- 2 tablespoons honey
- 2 tablespoons Dijon-style mustard
- 1/8 teaspoon ground cumin
- Shredded Napa cabbage (optional)
- Corn-Tomato Relish*
- 10 8- to 10-inch plain or flavored flour tortillas

1 Trim fat from meat. Sprinkle meat with salt and black pepper. For glaze, in a small bowl stir together honey, mustard, and cumin; set aside.

2 For a charcoal grill, arrange hot coals around a drip pan. Test for medium-hot heat above pan. Place meat on the grill rack over the drip pan. Grill, covered, for 30 to 35 minutes or until an instant-read thermometer registers 155°F, brushing with honey-mustard mixture the last 5 to 10 minutes of grilling. (For gas grill, preheat grill. Reduce heat to medium-high. Adjust for indirect cooking. Place meat on grill rack; cover and grill as above.) Cover meat and let stand 15 minutes (meat temperature will rise to 160°F). Slice meat into thin bite-size strips.

3 To serve, divide meat; cabbage, if desired; and Corn-Tomato Relish among tortillas. Roll up.

*Corn-Tomato Relish: Thaw one 16-ounce package frozen whole kernel corn; drain well and pat dry with paper towels or use 3 cups fresh whole kernel corn. In a large skillet, heat 2 tablespoons olive oil over medium heat. Add corn, 1/2 cup finely chopped red onion and/or green onions, 1/4 cup finely chopped celery or green sweet pepper, 1 teaspoon minced garlic, 3/4 teaspoon salt, 1/2 teaspoon ground cumin or chili powder, and 1/8 teaspoon cayenne or ground black pepper. Cook about 10 minutes or until vegetables are tender, stirring occasionally. Remove from heat. Stir in 3/4 cup finely chopped and seeded tomatoes, 1/4 cup snipped fresh parsley, 1/4 cup mayonnaise, and 1 tablespoon lime juice. Cover and chill for at least 1 hour or up to 24 hours.

Nutrition Facts per wrap: 323 cal., 12 g total fat (3 g sat. fat), 62 mg chol., 501 mg sodium, 30 g carbo., 2 g fiber, 23 g pro.

chicken wraps WITH SPANISH RICE

Each of these easy roll-ups provides a handful of Southwestern-style good eating.

Prep: 25 minutes
Marinate: 30 minutes
Grill: 12 minutes
Makes: 4 servings

- 8 ounces skinless, boneless chicken breast halves
- 2 tablespoons olive oil
- 2 tablespoons lime juice
- ½ teaspoon ground cumin
- ½ teaspoon dried oregano, crushed
- ¼ teaspoon salt
- Spanish Rice*
- 4 7- to 8-inch flavored or whole-wheat flour tortillas
- 1 avocado, seeded, peeled, and thinly sliced
- 2 tablespoons snipped fresh cilantro
- Salsa (optional)
- Dairy sour cream (optional)
- Lime wedges (optional)

1 Place chicken in a resealable plastic bag set in a shallow dish. For marinade, in a small bowl combine oil, lime juice, cumin, oregano, and salt. Pour over chicken; seal bag. Marinate in the refrigerator for 30 minutes, turning bag occasionally. Drain chicken, discarding marinade.

2 Meanwhile, prepare Spanish Rice.

3 For a charcoal grill, grill chicken on the rack of an uncovered grill directly over medium coals for 12 to 15 minutes or until chicken is no longer pink (170°), turning once halfway through grilling. Place tortillas on the grill rack directly over medium coals the last 1 to 2 minutes of grilling or until heated through, turning once. (For a gas grill, preheat grill. Reduce heat to medium. Place chicken on grill rack over heat. Cover and grill as above.)

4 Spread some of the hot Spanish Rice on each tortilla. Top with avocado slices and cilantro. Chop chicken and arrange on top of vegetables. Fold in sides of tortilla and roll up. If desired, serve with salsa, sour cream, and lime wedges.

*Spanish Rice: In a medium saucepan combine 1 cup chicken broth, ¾ cup mild chunky salsa, and ⅔ cup long grain rice. Bring to boiling; reduce heat. Simmer, covered, about 20 minutes or until the rice is tender and most of liquid is absorbed.

Nutrition Facts per serving: 388 cal., 15 g total fat (3 g sat. fat), 33 mg chol., 658 mg sodium, 45 g carbo., 3 g fiber, 19 g pro.

chicken
AND TURKEY

Chicken Stuffed with Spinach and Sweet Peppers, *recipe page 77*

zesty CURRY-LIME CHICKEN KABOBS

Prep: 20 minutes
Marinate: 4 to 24 hours
Grill: 15 minutes
Makes: 4 servings

- 1 pound skinless, boneless chicken breast halves, cut into 1½-inch pieces
- ½ cup plain yogurt
- ¼ cup snipped fresh cilantro
- 1 teaspoon finely shredded lime peel
- 2 tablespoons lime juice
- 2 tablespoons olive oil or cooking oil
- 1 tablespoon honey
- 1 tablespoon Dijon-style mustard
- 2 cloves garlic, minced
- ½ teaspoon curry powder
- ¼ teaspoon salt
- ¼ teaspoon black pepper
- 2 medium green and/or red sweet peppers, cut into 1-inch pieces
- 1 medium zucchini, cut into ½-inch slices
- 8 cherry tomatoes

1 Place chicken in a resealable plastic bag set in a shallow dish. For marinade, in a small bowl stir together yogurt, cilantro, lime peel, lime juice, oil, honey, mustard, garlic, curry powder, salt, and black pepper. Pour over chicken; seal bag. Marinate in the refrigerator for 4 to 24 hours, turning bag occasionally.

2 Drain chicken, reserving marinade. On eight long metal skewers, alternately thread chicken, sweet peppers, and zucchini, leaving a ¼-inch space between pieces. Brush vegetables with reserved marinade. Discard any remaining marinade.

3 For a charcoal grill, arrange medium-hot coals around a drip pan. Test for medium heat above the pan. Place kabobs on grill rack over drip pan. Cover; grill for 15 to 18 minutes or until chicken is no longer pink (170°F). Place a cherry tomato on the end of each skewer for the last 1 minute of grilling. (For a gas grill, preheat grill. Reduce heat to medium. Adjust for indirect cooking. Grill as above.)

Nutrition Facts per serving: 205 cal., 6 g total fat (1 g sat. fat), 67 mg chol., 200 mg sodium, 10 g carbo., 2 g fiber, 29 g pro.

chicken stuffed WITH SPINACH AND SWEET PEPPERS

Prep: 30 minutes
Marinate: 2 to 4 hours
Grill: 45 minutes
Makes: 6 servings

- 6 medium chicken breast halves (about 3 pounds)
- ¼ cup honey mustard
- 2 tablespoons mayonnaise or salad dressing
- 1 tablespoon olive oil
- 1 tablespoon red wine vinegar
- 1 teaspoon dried oregano, crushed
- 1 teaspoon dried basil, crushed
- 1 teaspoon dried rosemary, crushed
- 1 cup finely shredded mozzarella cheese (4 ounces)
- 1 cup chopped fresh spinach
- ½ cup finely chopped red sweet pepper
- ¼ teaspoon black pepper
- 3 cloves garlic, minced
- Grilled asparagus (optional)
- Roma tomatoes, cut up (optional)

1 Make a horizontal pocket in each chicken breast half by cutting from one side almost to but not through the other side. Place chicken in a resealable plastic bag set in a shallow dish. For marinade, in a small bowl combine mustard, mayonnaise, oil, vinegar, oregano, basil, and rosemary. Pour over chicken; seal bag. Marinate in the refrigerator for 2 to 4 hours, turning bag occasionally.

2 Meanwhile, for stuffing, in a medium bowl combine mozzarella cheese, spinach, sweet pepper, black pepper, and garlic. Spoon stuffing into pockets in chicken breast halves. If necessary, fasten pockets with wooden toothpicks.

3 For a charcoal grill, arrange medium-hot coals around a drip pan. Test for medium heat above pan. Place chicken breasts, bone sides down, on grill rack over drip pan. Cover; grill for 45 to 55 minutes or until chicken is no longer pink (170°F), turning once halfway through grilling. (For a gas grill, preheat grill. Reduce heat to medium. Adjust for indirect cooking. Grill as above.) If desired, serve with asparagus and tomatoes.

Nutrition Facts per serving: 297 cal., 11 g total fat (3 g sat. fat), 103 mg chol., 282 mg sodium, 5 g carbo., 1 g fiber, 41 g pro.

double CHERRY-CHICKEN ROLL-UPS

Sink your fork into one of these plump rolls and the creamy, cherry-dotted filling oozes out.

Prep: 30 minutes
Grill: 20 minutes
Makes: 4 servings

- ½ of an 8-ounce container mascarpone cheese or ½ of an 8-ounce tub (about ½ cup) cream cheese
- ⅓ cup snipped dried cherries
- 3 tablespoons thinly sliced green onions
- 4 skinless, boneless chicken breast halves
- 1 tablespoon packed brown sugar
- ½ teaspoon salt
- ¼ teaspoon black pepper
- Cherry-Orange Sauce*

1 For filling, in a small bowl combine mascarpone cheese, dried cherries, and green onions. Set filling aside.

2 Place each chicken breast half between two pieces of plastic wrap. Using the flat side of a meat mallet, pound the chicken lightly into rectangles about ¼ inch thick. Remove plastic wrap. Spread filling evenly over each chicken breast half to within ½ inch of edges. Fold in sides of each chicken piece; roll up from a short end. Secure with wooden toothpicks.

3 For rub, in a small bowl combine brown sugar, salt, and pepper. Sprinkle over chicken roll-ups; rub in with your fingers.

4 For a charcoal grill, arrange medium-hot coals around a drip pan. Test for medium heat above the pan. Place chicken on grill rack over drip pan. Cover; grill for 20 to 25 minutes or until chicken is no longer pink (170°F). (For a gas grill, preheat grill. Reduce heat to medium. Adjust for indirect cooking. Grill as above.)

5 Serve with Cherry-Orange Sauce.

***Cherry-Orange Sauce:** Finely shred enough peel from 1 orange to equal 1 teaspoon. Set aside. Peel and section the orange over a bowl to catch the juices. Add enough additional orange juice to equal ¼ cup. In a small saucepan combine ½ cup cherry preserves and the orange juice; heat and stir until melted. Remove from heat. Coarsely chop the orange sections; add to preserves mixture along with the 1 teaspoon peel.

Nutrition Facts per serving: 459 cal., 15 g total fat (8 g sat. fat), 118 mg chol., 400 mg sodium, 45 g carbo., 2 g fiber, 40 g pro.

grilled CHICKEN FETTUCCINE

Pesto and a rich, creamy sauce turn grilled chicken strips into an elegant entrée.

Prep: 20 minutes
Grill: 12 minutes
Makes: 6 servings

- 1 cup whipping cream
- ⅓ cup butter or margarine
- ¾ cup grated Parmesan cheese
- 4 skinless, boneless chicken breast halves
- 12 ounces dried fettuccine
- ¼ cup purchased pesto
- 1 cup cherry tomatoes, halved
- Dash black pepper
- Toasted pine nuts (optional)
- Snipped fresh basil (optional)

1 In a small saucepan heat whipping cream and butter until butter melts. Gradually add Parmesan cheese, stirring until combined. Cover and keep warm over low heat.

2 For a charcoal grill, grill chicken on the rack of an uncovered grill directly over medium coals for 12 to 15 minutes or until chicken is no longer pink (170°F), turning once halfway through grilling. (For a gas grill, preheat grill. Reduce heat to medium. Place chicken on grill rack over heat. Cover and grill as above.)

3 Meanwhile, cook fettuccine according to package directions. Drain and keep warm.

4 Cut grilled chicken into bite-size pieces. In a medium bowl toss chicken with 1 tablespoon of the pesto. Add remaining pesto and Parmesan mixture to the hot cooked fettuccine. Add tomatoes. Toss to coat. Arrange fettuccine on a serving platter; sprinkle with pepper. Top with grilled chicken. If desired, garnish with pine nuts and basil.

Nutrition Facts per serving: 673 cal., 38 g total fat (17 g sat. fat), 148 mg chol., 389 mg sodium, 47 g carbo., 2 g fiber, 36 g pro.

mushroom-stuffed CHICKEN

Tucked under the skin, Italian-scented mushrooms penetrate the chicken with flavor.

Prep: 30 minutes
Grill: 50 minutes
Stand: 10 minutes
Makes: 4 to 6 servings

- 2 tablespoons olive oil
- 1 to 1¼ pounds chopped mixed mushrooms (4 cups)
- 1 clove garlic, minced
- 2 teaspoons snipped fresh oregano or ¼ teaspoon dried oregano, crushed
- 2 tablespoons dry Marsala (optional)
- 1 teaspoon anchovy paste or soy sauce
- ¼ teaspoon salt
- ¼ teaspoon freshly ground black pepper
- 2½ to 3 pounds meaty chicken pieces (breast halves, thighs, and drumsticks)
- Salt and freshly ground black pepper
- Lemon halves (optional)
- Fresh oregano sprigs (optional)

1 In a large skillet heat olive oil over medium heat. Add mushrooms, garlic, and oregano. Cook until mushrooms are lightly browned and tender, 6 to 8 minutes, stirring occasionally. Remove from heat. Stir in Marsala (if desired), anchovy paste, ¼ teaspoon salt, and ¼ teaspoon pepper. Return to heat and cook and stir 2 minutes more. Remove from heat and allow to cool slightly, about 10 minutes.

2 With your hands, loosen skin of each chicken piece on one side. Stuff mushroom mixture evenly beneath the skin of each chicken piece. Sprinkle chicken lightly with salt and pepper.

3 For a charcoal grill, arrange medium-hot coals around a drip pan. Test for medium heat above the pan. Place chicken pieces, bone sides down, on the grill rack over drip pan. Grill, covered, for 50 to 60 minutes or until chicken is no longer pink (170°F for breast halves, 180°F for thighs and drumsticks). (For a gas grill, preheat grill. Reduce heat to medium. Adjust heat for indirect cooking. Place chicken pieces on the grill rack. Grill as above.)

4 If desired, serve with fresh lemon and garnish with oregano.

Nutrition Facts per serving: 328 cal., 16 g total fat (4 g sat. fat), 116 mg chol., 437 mg sodium, 4 g carbo., 1 g fiber, 41 g pro.

peach-glazed CHICKEN

Sweet peach preserves get a double kick of pungency from horseradish and fresh ginger to create a glitzy glaze impossible to forget.

Prep: 15 minutes
Grill: 50 minutes
Makes: 4 to 6 servings

- 2½ to 3 pounds meaty chicken pieces (breast halves, thighs, and drumsticks)
- Salt and coarsely ground black pepper
- ½ cup peach preserves, large pieces snipped
- 1 tablespoon white wine vinegar
- 1 tablespoon prepared horseradish
- 1 teaspoon freshly grated ginger
- ½ teaspoon salt
- ½ teaspoon coarsely ground black pepper

1 Remove the skin from chicken, if desired. Sprinkle chicken lightly with salt and pepper. For a charcoal grill, arrange preheated coals around a drip pan. Test for medium heat above the pan. Place chicken on the grill rack above the drip pan. Grill, covered, for 40 minutes. (For a gas grill, preheat grill. Reduce heat to medium. Adjust for indirect cooking. Place chicken on grill rack. Grill as above.)

2 Meanwhile, in a small microwave-safe bowl combine preserves, vinegar, horseradish, ginger, ½ teaspoon salt, and ½ teaspoon pepper. Microwave, uncovered, on 100% power (high) for 30 to 60 seconds or until preserves are melted, stirring once. Brush over chicken pieces. Cover and grill for 10 to 20 minutes more or until chicken is no longer pink (170°F in breast halves, 180°F in thighs or drumsticks), brushing occasionally with sauce.

3 Spoon any remaining preserve mixture over chicken.

Nutrition Facts per serving: 356 cal., 9 g total fat (3 g sat. fat), 115 mg chol., 565 mg sodium, 28 g carbo., 1 g fiber, 37 g pro.

finger-lickin' BARBECUED CHICKEN

Prep: 45 minutes
Marinate: 2 to 4 hours
Grill: 50 minutes
Makes: 6 servings

- 3 to 4 pounds meaty chicken pieces (breast halves, thighs, and drumsticks)
- 1½ cups dry sherry
- 1 cup finely chopped onion (1 large)
- ¼ cup lemon juice
- 2 bay leaves
- 6 cloves garlic, minced
- 1 15-ounce can tomato puree
- ¼ cup honey
- 3 tablespoons mild-flavored molasses
- 1 teaspoon salt
- ½ teaspoon dried thyme, crushed
- ¼ to ½ teaspoon cayenne pepper
- ¼ teaspoon black pepper
- 2 tablespoons white vinegar

1 Place chicken in a resealable plastic bag set in a shallow dish. For marinade, in a medium bowl stir together sherry, onion, lemon juice, bay leaves, and garlic. Pour over chicken; seal bag. Marinate in the refrigerator for 2 to 4 hours, turning bag occasionally. Drain chicken, reserving marinade.

2 Meanwhile, for sauce, in a large saucepan combine reserved marinade, tomato puree, honey, molasses, salt, thyme, cayenne pepper, and black pepper. Bring to boiling. Reduce heat and simmer, uncovered, about 30 minutes or until reduced to 2 cups. Remove from heat; remove bay leaves. Stir in vinegar.

3 For a charcoal grill, arrange medium-hot coals around a drip pan. Test for medium heat above the pan. Place chicken pieces, bone sides down, on grill rack over drip pan. Cover; grill for 50 to 60 minutes or until chicken is no longer pink (170°F for breasts, 180°F for thighs and drumsticks), brushing with some of the sauce during the last 15 minutes of grilling. (For a gas grill, preheat grill. Reduce heat to medium. Adjust for indirect cooking. Grill as above.) To serve, reheat the remaining sauce and pass with chicken.

Nutrition Facts per serving: 503 cal., 18 g total fat (5 g sat. fat), 129 mg chol., 779 mg sodium, 35 g carbo., 2 g fiber, 35 g pro.

orange-coriander GLAZED CHICKEN

Prep: 30 minutes
Grill: 35 minutes
Makes: 4 servings

- ⅓ cup orange marmalade
- 1 tablespoon soy sauce
- 1 tablespoon Oriental chili sauce
- 1½ teaspoons ground coriander
- 2½ pounds meaty chicken pieces (breast halves, thighs, and drumsticks)
- Salt and black pepper
- 1 orange, cut into thin wedges
- Snipped fresh cilantro (optional)

1 For glaze, in a small saucepan combine marmalade, soy sauce, chili sauce, and coriander; heat and stir over low heat until marmalade is melted. Set aside.

2 If desired, remove skin from chicken. Sprinkle chicken with salt and pepper. For a charcoal grill, grill chicken pieces, bone sides up, on the rack of an uncovered grill directly over medium coals for 35 to 45 minutes or until chicken is no longer pink (170°F for breasts, 180°F for thighs and drumsticks), turning once halfway through grilling and brushing occasionally with glaze during the last 10 minutes of grilling. (For a gas grill, preheat grill. Reduce heat to medium. Place chicken on grill rack over heat. Cover and grill as above.)

3 Serve with orange wedges. If desired, sprinkle chicken with cilantro.

Nutrition Facts per serving: 411 cal., 16 g total fat (4 g sat. fat), 130 mg chol., 670 mg sodium, 23 g carbo., 1 g fiber, 43 g pro.

mango-lime-sauced
CHICKEN THIGHS

With the tang of tropical fruit and a hint of pepper, the mango sauce enlivens chicken with complementary flavors.

Prep: 30 minutes
Grill: 50 minutes
Makes: 4 servings

- 8 chicken thighs
- ½ teaspoon salt
- ¼ teaspoon ground nutmeg
- ⅛ teaspoon cayenne pepper
- 1 large mango, peeled, pitted and cubed (about 1¼ cups)
- 2 tablespoons packed brown sugar
- 1 teaspoon finely shredded lime peel
- 1 tablespoon lime juice
- 2 teaspoons Worcestershire sauce
- ⅛ teaspoon cayenne pepper
- Mango wedges, lime slices, and sweet cherries (optional)

1 If desired, remove skin from chicken. Combine salt, nutmeg, and ⅛ teaspoon cayenne pepper. Sprinkle over chicken pieces; rub in with your fingers.

2 In a blender or food processor combine mango, brown sugar, lime peel, lime juice, Worcestershire sauce, and ⅛ teaspoon cayenne pepper. Blend or process until smooth; set aside.

3 For a charcoal grill, arrange medium-hot coals around a drip pan. Test for medium heat above pan. Place chicken pieces, bone sides up, on grill rack over drip pan. Cover; grill for 50 to 60 minutes or until chicken is no longer pink (180°F), turning once halfway through grilling and brushing with sauce during the last 10 minutes of grilling. (For a gas grill, preheat grill. Reduce heat to medium. Adjust for indirect cooking. Grill as above.) Serve with mango wedges, lime slices, and/or sweet cherries.

Nutrition Facts per serving: 450 cal., 27 g total fat (8 g sat. fat), 157 mg chol., 442 mg sodium, 17 g carbo., 1 g fiber, 33 g pro.

honey-dijon BARBECUED CHICKEN

A combination of wine, honey, and Dijon-style mustard gives grilled chicken quarters irresistible flavor.

Prep: 15 minutes
Marinate: 8 to 24 hours
Grill: 50 minutes
Makes: 4 servings

- 1 3-pound broiler-fryer chicken, quartered
- ½ cup white Zinfandel wine, apple juice, or cider
- ¼ cup olive oil or cooking oil
- ¼ cup honey
- ¼ cup Dijon-style mustard
- 4 cloves garlic, minced
- ½ teaspoon black pepper
- ¼ teaspoon salt
- **Grilled vegetables (optional)**

1 Place chicken in a resealable plastic bag set in a shallow dish. For marinade, in a bowl combine wine, oil, honey, mustard, garlic, pepper, and salt. Pour marinade over chicken; seal bag. Marinate in the refrigerator for 8 to 24 hours, turning bag occasionally.

2 Drain chicken, reserving marinade. For a charcoal grill, arrange medium-hot coals around a drip pan. Test for medium heat above pan. Place chicken pieces, bone sides down, on grill rack over drip pan. Cover and grill for 50 to 60 minutes or until chicken is no longer pink (170°F for breast portions; 180°F for thigh portions), brushing once with reserved marinade after 30 minutes of grilling. (For a gas grill, preheat grill. Reduce heat to medium. Adjust for indirect cooking. Grill as above.) Discard any remaining marinade.

3 If desired, serve with grilled vegetables.

Nutrition Facts per serving: 597 cal., 40 g total fat (10 g sat. fat), 172 mg chol., 384 mg sodium, 11 g carbo., 0 g fiber, 45 g pro.

sesame GRILLED CHICKEN

Soy sauce, sesame seeds, and fresh ginger lend an Asian touch. Serve the grilled chicken with jasmine, basmati, or other aromatic rice.

Prep: 25 minutes
Marinate: 3 to 4 hours
Grill: 50 minutes
Makes: 8 servings

- 2 2½- to 3-pound broiler-fryer chickens, quartered, or 5 to 6 pounds meaty chicken pieces (breasts, thighs, and drumsticks)
- ½ cup olive oil
- ½ cup dry white wine
- ½ cup soy sauce
- ½ cup chopped green onions (4)
- 3 tablespoons sesame seeds
- 4 cloves garlic, minced
- 1 tablespoon grated fresh ginger
- 1 teaspoon dry mustard
- 1 teaspoon freshly ground black pepper
- Steamed baby bok choy (optional)

1 If desired, remove skin from chicken. Place the chicken in resealable plastic bags set in shallow dishes.

2 For marinade, in a medium bowl combine oil, wine, soy sauce, green onions, sesame seeds, garlic, ginger, dry mustard, and pepper. Pour marinade over chicken; seal bags. Marinate in the refrigerator for 3 to 4 hours, turning bag occasionally.

3 Drain chicken, reserving marinade. For a charcoal grill, arrange medium-hot coals around a drip pan. Test for medium heat above the pan. Place chicken pieces, bone sides down, on grill rack over drip pan. Cover; grill for 50 to 60 minutes or until chicken is no longer pink (170°F for breast portions; 180°F for thigh portions), turning once and brushing frequently with about half of the reserved marinade during the first 35 minutes of grilling. (For a gas grill, preheat grill. Reduce heat to medium. Adjust for indirect cooking. Grill as above.) Discard any remaining marinade.

4 If desired, serve with baby bok choy.

Nutrition Facts per serving: 486 cal., 36 g total fat (9 g sat. fat), 144 mg chol., 570 mg sodium, 1 g carbo., 0 g fiber, 37 g pro.

game hens WITH RHUBARB BARBECUE GLAZE

Bottled barbecue sauce becomes worthy of Cornish hens when simmered with chopped rhubarb. The tangy mixture provides a spectacular glaze.

Prep: 30 minutes
Cook: 20 minutes
Roast: 55 minutes
Makes: 6 servings

- 3½ to 4 cups chopped fresh or frozen rhubarb
- 1 cup bottled tomato-based barbecue sauce
- ¼ cup water
- 3 1¼- to 1½-pound Cornish game hens
- Olive oil
- Salt and black pepper
- 8 ounces dried orzo (rosamarina)
- 1 cup packaged shredded carrots
- ¼ cup sliced green onions (2)
- Salt and black pepper

1 For sauce, in a medium saucepan combine rhubarb, barbecue sauce, and water; bring to boiling over medium-high heat. Reduce heat to medium-low and cook, covered, for 20 minutes or until the rhubarb loses its shape. Remove from the heat and coarsely mash the rhubarb in the pan. Remove and reserve 1 cup of the sauce.

2 Use a long, heavy knife or kitchen shears to halve Cornish hens lengthwise, cutting through the breast bone, just off-center, and through the center of the backbone. (Or ask the butcher to cut hens into halves.) Twist wing tips under back. Rub surface and cavity of each hen half with oil; sprinkle generously with salt and pepper.

3 For a charcoal grill, arrange medium-hot coals around a drip pan. Test for medium heat above pan. Place hens, bone sides down, on rack over drip pan. Cover; grill for 40 to 50 minutes or until no longer pink, brushing with some of the remaining sauce during the last 15 minutes or grilling. (For a gas grill, preheat grill. Reduce heat to medium. Adjust for indirect cooking. Grill as above.)

4 Meanwhile, cook orzo according to package directions; drain. In a large bowl stir together orzo, the 1 cup reserved sauce, carrots, and green onions. Season to taste with salt and pepper. Serve hens with orzo mixture and remaining sauce.

Nutrition Facts per serving: 375 cal., 10 g total fat (2 g sat. fat), 111 mg chol., 609 mg sodium, 39 g carbo., 4 g fiber, 31 g pro.

tahini TURKEY THIGHS

Rich-flavored tahini is the color of peanut butter, but much thicker. Use a whisk when combining it with the other ingredients.

Prep: 45 minutes
Grill: 50 minutes
Makes: 6 servings

- 4 turkey thighs (about 3½ to 4 pounds)
- ½ cup tahini (sesame seed paste)
- ¼ cup water
- 2 tablespoons soy sauce
- 1 tablespoon lemon juice
- 1 tablespoon honey
- 1 tablespoon Asian chili garlic sauce
- 1 teaspoon grated fresh ginger
- Chickpea Salad*

1 If desired, remove skin from turkey. For sauce, in a medium bowl whisk together tahini, water, soy sauce, lemon juice, honey, chili garlic sauce, and ginger until combined; set aside.

2 For a charcoal grill, arrange medium-hot coals around a drip pan. Test for medium heat above the pan. Place turkey highs, bone-sides up, on grill rack over drip pan. Cover; grill for 50 to 60 minutes or until turkey is no longer pink (180°F), turning once halfway through grilling and brushing frequently with sauce during the last 20 minutes of grilling. (For a gas grill, preheat grill. Reduce heat to medium. Adjust for indirect cooking. Grill as above.) Discard any remaining sauce.

3 To serve, cut turkey meat from bones. Serve with Chickpea Salad.

*Chickpea Salad: In a small screwtop jar combine 3 tablespoons olive oil, 3 tablespoons lemon juice, ¼ teaspoon salt, and ⅛ teaspoon black pepper. Cover and shake well. Rinse and drain two 15-ounce cans garbanzo beans. In a large bowl combine the beans; ¾ cup finely chopped yellow or red sweet pepper; ⅔ cup snipped fresh parsley; ½ cup finely chopped, seeded cucumber; ⅓ cup snipped fresh mint; 2 chopped, seeded roma tomatoes; and ¼ cup finely chopped red onion. Add dressing; toss to combine. Cover and chill until ready to serve.

Nutrition Facts per serving: 600 cal., 32 g total fat (6 g sat. fat), 119 mg chol., 985 mg sodium, 34 g carbo., 8 g fiber, 44 g pro.

orange-balsamic TURKEY TENDERLOINS

Less is more in this case. To be sure the turkey stays juicy and tender, refrigerate it in the brine no longer than 6 hours.

Prep: 10 minutes
Marinate: 4 to 6 hours
Grill: 12 minutes
Makes: 4 servings

- 2 turkey breast tenderloins
- ½ cup balsamic vinegar
- 2 cups orange juice
- 3 tablespoons coarse kosher salt
- 1 tablespoon sugar
- 1 tablespoon dried basil, crushed
- ½ teaspoon ground black pepper
- ¼ cup orange marmalade

1 Split each tenderloin in half horizontally. Set aside 1 tablespoon of the vinegar. For brine, in a large bowl combine remaining vinegar, the orange juice, salt, sugar, basil, and pepper. Place tenderloins in brine mixture. Cover and marinate in the refrigerator for at least 4 hours or up to 6 hours, turning tenderloins occasionally.

2 Drain tenderloins; discard brine. Rinse tenderloins and pat dry with paper towels. In a small bowl combine the reserved vinegar and marmalade.

3 For a charcoal grill, place tenderloins on the grill rack directly over medium coals. Grill, uncovered, for 12 to 15 minutes or until turkey is no longer pink (170°F), turning once halfway through grilling and brushing with marmalade mixture during the last 2 minutes of grilling. (For a gas grill, preheat grill. Reduce heat to medium. Place tenderloins on grill rack over heat. Cover and grill as above.)

Nutrition Facts per serving: 364 cal., 18 g fat (6 g sat. fat), 119 mg chol., 577 mg sodium, 8 g carbo., 2 g fiber, 41 g pro.

turkey breast STUFFED WITH SAUSAGE, FENNEL, AND FIGS

Prep: 20 minutes
Grill: 1½ hours
Stand: 10 minutes
Makes: 10 to 12 servings

- 1 4- to 5-pound bone-in turkey breast
- ½ teaspoon salt
- ½ teaspoon ground black pepper
- 1 pound bulk or link sweet Italian sausage
- 12 green onions, thinly sliced
- ⅔ cup snipped dried figs
- 1½ teaspoons fennel seeds
- 2 tablespoons olive oil
- ¼ teaspoon salt
- ¼ teaspoon ground black pepper

1 Remove bone from turkey (you may want to ask the butcher to remove the bone for you). Place turkey, skin side down, between two pieces of plastic wrap. Working from the center to the edges, pound lightly with the flat side of a meat mallet to an even thickness. Remove plastic wrap. Sprinkle turkey with the ½ teaspoon salt and the ½ teaspoon pepper.

2 For stuffing, remove casings from sausage, if present. In a medium bowl combine sausage, green onions, figs, and fennel seeds.

3 Spoon stuffing over half of the turkey; fold other half of turkey over stuffing. Tie in several places with 100-percent-cotton kitchen string or secure with metal skewers. Rub skin with oil and sprinkle with the ¼ teaspoon salt and the ¼ teaspoon pepper.

4 For a charcoal grill, arrange medium-hot coals around a drip pan in a grill with a cover. Test for medium heat above pan. Place turkey on the grill rack over pan. Cover and grill for 1½ to 2 hours or until turkey is no longer pink (170°F) and center of stuffing registers 165°F. (For a gas grill, preheat grill. Reduce heat to medium. Adjust for indirect cooking. Cover and grill as above.)

5 Remove turkey from grill. Cover with foil and let stand for 10 minutes before carving.

Nutrition Facts per serving: 364 cal., 18 g total fat (6 g sat. fat), 119 mg chol., 577 mg sodium, 8 g carbo., 2 g fiber, 41 g pro.

turkey FAJITAS

Pile the ingredients on the tortillas and serve the fajitas ready-made or lay out the makings on a platter and let diners assemble their own.

Prep: 20 minutes
Marinate: 1 hour
Grill: 12 minutes
Makes: 4 servings

- 12 ounces boneless turkey breast
- 1 cup bottled green taco sauce or green salsa (salsa verde)
- 2 tablespoons olive oil
- 10 8-inch flour tortillas
- 1 medium red onion, cut into ½-inch slices
- 2 medium zucchini and/or yellow summer squash, cut lengthwise into ½-inch slices
- 1 medium red sweet pepper, quartered and seeded
- Bottled green taco sauce or green salsa (salsa verde)
- Snipped fresh cilantro

1 Cut turkey into ½-inch slices. Place turkey in a resealable plastic bag set in a shallow dish. For marinade, in a small bowl combine the 1 cup taco sauce and oil. Pour ½ cup of marinade over turkey; seal bag. Marinate in the refrigerator for 1 hour, turning bag once. Reserve remaining marinade. Stack tortillas and wrap in foil.

2 Drain turkey, discarding marinade. Skewer onion slices with wooden toothpicks, inserting from one edge to the center. Brush onion, squash, and sweet pepper with reserved marinade.

3 For a charcoal grill, grill turkey and vegetables on the rack of an uncovered grill directly over medium coals for 12 to 14 minutes or until turkey is no longer pink (170°F), turning once halfway through grilling. Place tortilla packet on grill for the last 5 minutes of grilling. (For a gas grill, preheat grill. Reduce heat to medium. Place turkey, vegetables, and tortillas on grill rack over heat. Cover and grill as above.)

4 Cut turkey and vegetables into bite-size strips. On each tortilla arrange turkey, onion, squash, and red pepper; drizzle with taco sauce; and sprinkle with cilantro. Fold in sides; roll up tortillas.

Nutrition Facts per serving: 430 cal., 13 g total fat (3 g sat. fat), 53 mg chol., 573 mg sodium, 48 g carbo., 3 g fiber, 27 g pro.

pork

Double Peanut-Crusted Chops, *recipe page 110*

greek HONEY-LEMON PORK CHOPS

Prep: 15 minutes
Marinate: 4 to 24 hours
Grill: 11 minutes
Makes: 4 servings

- 4 bone-in pork rib chops, cut ¾ to 1 inch thick
- 2 tablespoons honey
- 2 teaspoons finely shredded lemon peel
- 2 tablespoons lemon juice
- 1 tablespoon snipped fresh mint or ½ teaspoon dried mint, crushed
- 1 tablespoon olive oil
- ½ teaspoon salt
- ¼ teaspoon cayenne pepper

1 Trim fat from chops. Place chops in a resealable plastic bag set in a shallow dish.

2 For marinade, in a small bowl combine honey, lemon peel, lemon juice, mint, oil, salt, and cayenne pepper. Pour over chops. Seal bag; turn to coat chops. Marinate in the refrigerator for 4 to 24 hours, turning bag occasionally. Drain chops, discarding marinade.

3 For a charcoal grill, place chops on the rack of an uncovered grill directly over medium coals. Grill for 11 to 13 minutes or until chops are slightly pink in center and juices run clear (160°F), turning once halfway through grilling. (For a gas grill, preheat grill. Reduce heat to medium. Place chops on grill rack over heat. Cover and grill as above.)

Nutrition Facts per serving: 257 cal., 11 g total fat (3 g sat. fat), 71 mg chol., 350 mg sodium, 10 g carbo., 0 g fiber, 29 g pro.

grilled YOGURT-MARINATED PORK CHOPS

Prep: 20 minutes
Marinate: 24 hours
Grill: 35 minutes
Makes: 4 servings

- 4 bone-in pork rib chops, cut 1¼ to 1½ inches thick
- 1½ cups plain low-fat yogurt
- ¼ cup snipped fresh cilantro
- 3 tablespoons finely chopped onion
- 3 tablespoons lemon juice
- 2 teaspoons ground coriander
- 4 cloves garlic, minced
- 1½ teaspoons salt
- 1 teaspoon ground cumin
- 1 teaspoon ground turmeric
- 1 teaspoon paprika
- 1 teaspoon dried marjoram, crushed
- 1 teaspoon freshly ground black pepper
- ¼ teaspoon thread saffron or ⅛ teaspoon ground saffron (optional)

1 Trim fat from chops. Place chops in a resealable plastic bag set in a shallow dish.

2 For marinade: in a medium bowl combine yogurt, cilantro, onion, lemon juice, coriander, garlic, salt, cumin, turmeric, paprika, marjoram, pepper, and, if desired, saffron. Pour over chops. Seal bag; turn to coat chops.

3 Marinate in the refrigerator for 24 hours, turning bag occasionally. Remove chops from marinade, scraping off and discarding excess marinade.

4 For a charcoal grill, arrange medium-hot coals around a drip pan in a grill with a cover. Test for medium heat above pan. Place chops on the grill rack over pan. Cover and grill for 35 to 40 minutes or until chops are slightly pink in center and juices run clear (160°F), turning once halfway through grilling. (For a gas grill, preheat grill. Reduce heat to medium. Adjust for indirect cooking. Cover and grill as above.)

Nutrition Facts per serving: 218 cal., 8 g total fat (3 g sat. fat), 73 mg chol., 372 mg sodium, 3 g carbo., 0 g fiber, 30 g pro.

beer-brined PORK LOIN CHOPS

Prep: 15 minutes
Marinate: 8 to 24 hours
Grill: 30 minutes
Makes: 4 servings

- 4 boneless pork top loin chops, cut 1½ inches thick
- 1¾ cups water
- 1¾ cups stout (dark beer)
- 3 tablespoons coarse salt
- 2 tablespoons mild-flavor molasses
- 2 teaspoons coarsely cracked black pepper
- 4 cloves garlic, minced

1 Trim fat from chops. Place chops in a resealable plastic bag set in a shallow dish. For beer brine, in a large bowl combine the water, stout, salt, and molasses; stir until salt is dissolved. Pour beer brine over chops; seal bag. Marinate in the refrigerator for 8 to 24 hours, turning bag occasionally.

2 Drain chops, discarding beer brine. Pat chops dry with paper towels. In a small bowl combine pepper and garlic. Sprinkle pepper mixture evenly over both sides of each chop; rub in with your fingers.

3 For a charcoal grill, arrange medium-hot coals around a drip pan in a grill with a cover. Test for medium heat above pan. Place chops on the grill rack over pan. Cover and grill for 30 to 35 minutes or until chops are slightly pink in center and juices run clear (160°F), turning once halfway through grilling. (For a gas grill, preheat grill. Reduce heat to medium. Adjust for indirect cooking. Cover and grill as above.)

Nutrition Facts per serving: 345 cal., 12 g total fat (4 g sat. fat), 123 mg chol., 702 mg sodium, 3 g carbo., 0 g fiber, 50 g pro.

mushroom-stuffed PORK CHOPS

The only thing better than a grilled pork chop is a grilled stuffed pork chop.

Prep: 25 minutes
Grill: 35 minutes
Makes: 4 servings

- ½ cup coarsely chopped fresh mushrooms (such as button, chanterelle, or shiitake)
- ¼ cup chopped onion
- 1 tablespoon butter or margarine
- 1 teaspoon grated fresh ginger
- ¼ teaspoon salt
- ¼ teaspoon black pepper
- 1 cup coarsely chopped fresh spinach
- ¼ cup soft bread crumbs
- 4 pork loin chops or pork rib chops, cut 1¼ inches thick
- ¼ cup ginger jelly or preserves or orange marmalade

1 For stuffing, in a saucepan cook mushrooms and onion in hot butter until onion is tender. Remove saucepan from heat; stir in ginger, salt, and pepper. Add spinach and bread crumbs, tossing gently until combined.

2 Trim fat from chops. Make a pocket in each chop by cutting horizontally from the fat side almost to the bone. Spoon one-fourth of the stuffing into each pocket. Secure openings with wooden toothpicks. Sprinkle chops with additional salt and black pepper.

3 For a charcoal grill, arrange medium-hot coals around a drip pan. Test for medium heat above pan. Place chops on grill rack over pan. Cover; grill for 35 to 40 minutes or until chops are slightly pink in center and juices run clear (160°F), turning once and brushing occasionally with ginger jelly during the last 5 minutes of grilling. (For a gas grill, preheat grill. Reduce heat to medium. Adjust for indirect cooking. Grill as above.)

Nutrition Facts per serving: 375 cal., 14 g total fat (5 g sat. fat), 114 mg chol., 268 mg sodium, 16 g carbo., 1 g fiber, 43 g pro.

pork CHOP AND POTATO DINNER

Foil-wrapped chops cook to a surprisingly tender degree.

Prep: 30 minutes
Grill: 30 minutes
Makes: 4 servings

- 8 tiny new potatoes, halved
- 1 medium red onion, thinly sliced and separated into rings
- 4 boneless pork loin chops, cut ¾ inch thick
- Salt
- Black pepper
- 1 medium red sweet pepper, cut into thin bite-size strips
- 2 medium carrots or 1 medium rutabaga, peeled and cut into thin bite-size strips
- ½ cup reduced-sodium chicken broth
- ½ teaspoon dry mustard
- ¼ teaspoon dried thyme, crushed

1 Divide new potatoes among four pieces of 18x12-inch heavy foil. Top each with a few of the onion rings. Trim fat from chops. Sprinkle chops with salt and pepper. Lay chops on top of onion rings. Top each chop with a few of the remaining onion rings, the sweet pepper strips, and carrot strips.

2 In a bowl combine chicken broth, mustard, and thyme. Drizzle 2 tablespoons of the broth mixture over each pork chop. Bring up two opposite edges of foil and seal with a double fold. Fold remaining edges together to completely enclose the pork chops and vegetables, leaving space for steam to build.

3 For a charcoal grill, grill foil packets on the rack of an uncovered grill directly over medium coals for 30 to 35 minutes or until chops are slightly pink in center and juices run clear (160°F) and vegetables are tender, turning packets twice. (For a gas grill, preheat grill. Reduce heat to medium. Place foil packets on grill rack over heat. Cover and grill as above.)

Nutrition Facts per serving: 281 cal., 7 g total fat (2 g sat. fat), 62 mg chol., 283 mg sodium, 24 g carbo., 4 g fiber, 29 g pro.

summer pork chops WITH CORN-MANGO SALSA

When combined with a few other ingredients, the snappy combination of corn and mango makes a tantalizing topper for blackened chops.

Prep: 40 minutes
Marinate: 12 hours
Grill: 14 minutes
Makes: 6 servings

- ⅓ cup olive oil
- 2 tablespoons blackened steak seasoning
- 2 teaspoons garlic powder
- 1 large onion, thinly sliced
- 6 boneless pork loin chops, cut 1 inch thick
- Corn-Mango Salsa*
- Steamed green and yellow beans (optional)

1 For marinade, in a heavy, resealable plastic bag combine oil, steak seasoning, and garlic powder; mix well. Add onion; mix well. Add chops; seal bag and turn to coat chops. Place bag in a large bowl. Marinate in the refrigerator for 12 hours or overnight, turning bag occasionally. Drain chops; discard marinade.

2 For a charcoal grill, place chops on the grill rack directly over medium heat. Grill, uncovered, for 14 to 18 minutes or until chops are slightly pink in center and juices run clear (160°F), turning once halfway through grilling. (For a gas grill, preheat grill. Reduce heat to medium. Place chops on the grill rack over heat. Cover and grill as above.) Serve chops with Corn-Mango Salsa and, if desired, green and yellow beans.

***Corn-Mango Salsa:** Husk 2 ears fresh sweet corn and brush with olive oil, coating all kernels. Place corn on the grill rack directly over medium heat. Grill, uncovered, until kernels are tender and just begin to brown, turning often. Remove ears from grill; cool. Cut kernels from ears. In a medium bowl, combine corn kernels; 1 medium mango, seeded, peeled, and finely chopped; ½ cup finely chopped red sweet pepper; ¼ cup chopped sweet onion; ¼ cup fresh lemon juice; 2 tablespoons cooking oil; 2 tablespoons snipped fresh mint; 1 tablespoon snipped fresh cilantro; and ¼ teaspoon salt. Toss gently to mix.

Nutrition Facts per serving: 479 cal., 22 g total fat (4 g sat. fat), 124 mg chol., 758 mg sodium, 17 g carbo., 2 g fiber, 53 g pro.

chops IN SMOKY CHILE MARINADE

The indispensable ingredient in this marinade is smoky chipotle chile peppers. Canned chipotles are packed in a piquant sauce made from chiles, herbs, and vinegar.

Prep: 20 minutes
Marinate: 4 hours
Grill: 11 minutes
Makes: 4 servings

- 4 pork loin butterfly chops, cut ¾ inch thick
- 3 tablespoons olive oil
- ½ teaspoon finely shredded lime peel
- 2 tablespoons lime juice
- 2 tablespoons finely chopped canned chipotle peppers in adobo sauce
- 1½ teaspoons dried oregano, crushed
- 1 teaspoon salt
- 3 cloves garlic, minced

1 Trim fat from chops. Place chops in a resealable plastic bag set in a shallow dish. For marinade, in a small bowl combine olive oil, lime peel, lime juice, chipotle peppers, oregano, salt, and garlic. Pour over chops; seal bag. Marinate in refrigerator for 4 hours, turning bag occasionally.

2 Drain chops, discarding marinade. For a charcoal grill, grill chops on the rack of an uncovered grill directly over medium coals for 11 to 13 minutes or until slightly pink in center and juices run clear (160°F), turning once halfway through grilling. (For a gas grill, preheat grill. Reduce heat to medium. Place meat on grill rack over heat. Cover and grill as above.)

Nutrition Facts per serving: 433 cal., 23 g total fat (6 g sat. fat), 123 mg chol., 709 mg sodium, 2 g carbo., 0 g fiber, 50 g pro.

double PEANUT-CRUSTED CHOPS

Keep the grill cover handy for this one. For the best results, cover the grill after adding the peanut crust so it gets slightly crispy.

Prep: 15 minutes
Grill: 11 minutes
Makes: 4 servings

- ⅓ cup creamy peanut butter
- ⅓ cup pineapple juice
- 2 tablespoons finely chopped green onion (1)
- 1 tablespoon soy sauce
- 1 tablespoon honey
- 1 teaspoon grated fresh ginger or ¼ teaspoon ground ginger
- ½ teaspoon dry mustard
- Several dashes bottled hot pepper sauce
- ⅓ cup finely chopped honey-roasted peanuts
- 2 tablespoons fine dry bread crumbs
- 1 tablespoon toasted sesame seeds
- 4 boneless pork sirloin chops, cut ¾ inch thick
- 4 ounces Chinese egg noodles or dried angel hair pasta

1 For peanut sauce, in a small saucepan heat peanut butter until melted; gradually whisk in pineapple juice, green onion, soy sauce, honey, ginger, mustard, and hot pepper sauce. Set aside 2 tablespoons of the peanut sauce. Keep remaining peanut sauce warm. For crust, in a small bowl combine peanuts, bread crumbs, and sesame seeds; set aside.

2 For a charcoal grill, grill chops on the rack of an uncovered grill directly over medium coals for 6 minutes. Turn chops and brush with the reserved 2 tablespoons peanut sauce. Sprinkle chops with crust mixture. With the back of a metal spatula, press crust onto chops. Cover and grill for 5 to 7 minutes more or until chops are slightly pink in center and juices run clear (160°F). (For a gas grill, preheat grill. Reduce heat to medium. Place chops on grill rack over heat. Cover and grill as above.)

3 Meanwhile, cook noodles according to package directions; drain. Toss noodles with the remaining peanut sauce. Serve with chops.

Nutrition Facts per serving: 510 cal., 23 g total fat (5 g sat. fat), 89 mg chol., 518 mg sodium, 39 g carbo., 6 g fiber, 42 g pro.

asian APRICOT-GLAZED CHOPS

A little goes a long way. Handle the extra spicy Oriental chili-garlic sauce the same way you would hot pepper sauce.

Prep: 15 minutes
Grill: 11 minutes
Makes: 4 servings

- ⅓ cup apricot preserves
- 1 tablespoon Oriental chili-garlic sauce
- 2 teaspoons soy sauce
- ¼ teaspoon ground ginger
- 4 boneless pork sirloin chops, cut ¾ inch thick
- Salt
- Ground black pepper

1 For the glaze, place apricot preserves in a small bowl; snip any large pieces of fruit. Stir in chili-garlic sauce, soy sauce, and ginger. Set glaze aside. Sprinkle both sides of each chop with salt and pepper.

2 For a charcoal grill, place chops on the grill rack directly over medium coals. Grill, uncovered, for 11 to 13 minutes or until chops are slightly pink in center and juices run clear (160°F), turning once halfway through grilling and brushing with glaze during the last 2 to 3 minutes of grilling. (For a gas grill, preheat grill. Reduce heat to medium. Place chops on the grill rack over heat. Cover and grill as above.)

Nutrition Facts per serving: 317 cal., 9 g total fat (3 g sat. fat), 106 mg chol., 515 mg sodium, 20 g carbo., 0 g fiber, 36 g pro.

fennel pork WITH ORZO RISOTTO

Use the vegetables that are grilled alongside the pork roast as a colorful addition to the risotto.

Prep: 25 minutes
Marinate: 4 to 24 hours
Grill: 1 hour
Stand: 15 minutes
Makes: 4 servings

- 1 2- to 2½-pound boneless pork top loin roast (single loin)
- 2 tablespoons fennel seeds, crushed
- 2 tablespoons balsamic vinegar
- 1 tablespoon finely shredded orange peel
- 2 tablespoons orange juice
- ¼ teaspoon salt
- ¼ teaspoon black pepper
- 4 cloves garlic, halved
- ¼ cup olive oil
- 1 small red sweet pepper, quartered lengthwise
- 1 small zucchini, quartered lengthwise
- 3 cups chicken broth
- ⅓ cup chopped onion (1 small)
- 1 tablespoon olive oil
- 1 cup orzo
- 2 tablespoons finely shredded Parmesan cheese

1 Trim fat from meat. Place meat in a resealable plastic bag set in a shallow dish. For marinade, in a food processor or blender combine fennel seeds, balsamic vinegar, orange peel, orange juice, salt, pepper, and garlic. Cover and process or blend until combined. With machine running, gradually add the ¼ cup oil, processing until smooth. Pour over meat; seal bag. Marinate in refrigerator for 4 to 24 hours.

2 Drain meat, discarding marinade. For a charcoal grill, arrange medium coals around a drip pan. Test for medium-low heat above pan. Place meat on grill rack over drip pan. Cover; grill for 1 to 1½ hours or until a meat thermometer registers 155°F. Place sweet peppers, skin sides down, and zucchini on grill rack directly over the coals. Grill sweet peppers about 8 minutes and zucchini for 5 to 6 minutes or until tender, turning once. Remove vegetables from grill. Chop vegetables; set aside to use in risotto. (For a gas grill, preheat grill. Reduce heat to medium-low. Adjust for indirect cooking. Grill as above, except place meat on a rack in a roasting pan.)

3 Meanwhile, for risotto, in a medium saucepan bring chicken broth to boiling. Cover and reduce heat until broth just simmers. In a large nonstick skillet cook onion in the 1 tablespoon hot oil until tender. Add orzo; cook and stir for 1 minute more. Carefully add ½ cup of the hot broth to orzo mixture, stirring constantly. Cook and stir over medium heat until broth is absorbed. Continue adding broth, ½ cup at a time, stirring constantly until broth has been absorbed but mixture is creamy. (This should take about 16 minutes total.) Remove from heat. Stir in chopped grilled vegetables and Parmesan cheese.

4 Remove meat from grill. Cover with foil and let stand 15 minutes. (The meat's temperature will rise 5°F during standing.) Serve roast with risotto.

Nutrition Facts per serving: 752 cal., 34 g total fat (9 g sat. fat), 154 mg chol., 1,322 mg sodium, 42 g carbo., 3 g fiber, 65 g pro.

caribbean pork WITH THREE-PEPPER SALSA

A prismatic salsa accompanies citrus-marinated grilled pork roast for a picture-perfect presentation.

Prep: 25 minutes
Marinate: 6 to 8 hours
Grill: 1 hour
Stand: 15 minutes
Makes: 6 to 8 servings

- 1 cup orange juice
- 2 teaspoons finely shredded lime peel
- ¼ cup lime juice
- ¼ cup cooking oil
- ½ cup chopped green onions (4)
- 2 tablespoons soy sauce
- 1 tablespoon grated fresh ginger
- 2 fresh serrano chile peppers, seeded and finely chopped
- 2 cloves garlic, minced
- 1 2- to 2½-pound boneless pork top loin roast (single loin)
- 1 medium green sweet pepper, quartered lengthwise
- 1 medium yellow or orange sweet pepper, quartered lengthwise
- ½ cup cherry tomatoes, quartered
- 2 tablespoons snipped fresh cilantro

1 For marinade, in a small bowl combine orange juice, lime peel, lime juice, oil, ¼ cup of the green onions, soy sauce, ginger, chile peppers, and garlic. Reserve 2 tablespoons of the marinade for the salsa; cover and chill until needed.

2 Trim fat from meat. Place meat in a resealable plastic bag set in a shallow dish. Pour remaining marinade over meat; seal bag. Marinate in refrigerator for 6 to 8 hours, turning bag occasionally.

3 Drain pork, discarding marinade. For a charcoal grill, arrange medium coals around a drip pan. Test for medium-low heat above pan. Place meat on grill rack over drip pan. Cover; grill for 1 to 1½ hours or until a meat thermometer registers 155°F. Place sweet peppers, skin sides down, on grill rack directly over the coals. Grill about 10 minutes or until skin is charred. Wrap pepper quarters in foil. Let stand until cool enough to handle. Use a sharp knife to gently and slowly peel off the skin. Discard skin. Chop peppers. (For a gas grill, preheat grill. Reduce heat to medium-low. Adjust for indirect cooking. Grill as above, except place meat on a rack in a roasting pan.)

4 For salsa, in a medium bowl combine the reserved marinade, chopped grilled sweet peppers, the remaining ¼ cup green onions, cherry tomatoes, and cilantro.

5 Remove meat from grill. Cover with foil and let stand 15 minutes. The temperature of the meat after standing should be 160°F. Serve with salsa.

Nutrition Facts per serving: 297 cal., 14 g total fat (4 g sat. fat), 82 mg chol., 212 mg sodium, 7 g carbo., 1 g fiber, 34 g pro.

grilled pork WITH MELON-TOMATO TUMBLE

Although the colorful pear-shape tomatoes make a stunning statement here, chopped plum tomatoes work well too.

Prep: 20 minutes
Grill: 30 minutes
Stand: 10 minutes
Makes: 4 servings

- 3 tablespoons olive oil
- 3 tablespoons white wine vinegar
- ¼ teaspoon salt
- ⅛ teaspoon black pepper
- 1 pound pork tenderloin
- ½ of a small cantaloupe
- ½ of a small honeydew melon
- 1 cup yellow, red, and/or orange pear-shape tomatoes, halved or quartered
- 1 small red onion, halved and thinly sliced
- ⅓ cup fresh mint leaves

1 In a small bowl whisk together oil, vinegar, salt, and pepper. Brush 1 tablespoon of the oil-and-vinegar mixture over the tenderloin. Reserve the remaining oil-and-vinegar mixture to use in the tumble.

2 For a charcoal grill, arrange hot coals around a drip pan. Test for medium-high heat above pan. Place meat on grill rack over pan. Cover; grill for 30 to 35 minutes or until a meat thermometer registers 155°F. Remove meat from grill. Cover with foil and let stand 10 minutes. (The meats temperature will rise 5°F during standing.)

3 Meanwhile, for tumble, cut either the cantaloupe or honeydew melon half into bite-size pieces. Cut the remaining melon half into 4 wedges. In a medium bowl combine the melon pieces, tomatoes, onion, and mint. Add the reserved oil-and-vinegar mixture; toss to coat.

4 Slice pork diagonally. Serve with the tumble spooned over the melon wedges.

Nutrition Facts per serving: 292 cal., 14 g total fat (3 g sat. fat), 73 mg chol., 211 mg sodium, 15 g carbo., 2 g fiber, 26 g pro.

prosciutto PORK KABOBS

To hold the proscuitto in place on the skewers, thread the skewers through the pork cubes in the spot where the prosciutto strips meet.

Prep: 20 minutes
Grill: 18 minutes
Makes: 4 servings

- ¼ cup garlic-flavored olive oil
- 2 tablespoons lemon juice
- ¼ teaspoon crushed red pepper
- 1 pound pork tenderloin
- 3 to 4 ounces thinly sliced prosciutto
- 8 ounces fresh mushrooms, stems removed
- 2 small zucchini and/or yellow summer squash, cut into ¾-inch-thick slices
- 2 tablespoons finely shredded Parmesan or Romano cheese

1 In a small bowl combine oil, lemon juice, and crushed red pepper; set aside.

2 Trim fat from pork. Cut pork into 1½-inch cubes. Cut proscuitto into 1½-inch-wide strips. Wrap a strip of proscuitto around each pork cube. On four long metal skewers, alternately thread pork cubes, mushrooms, and zucchini, leaving a ¼-inch space between pieces.

3 For a charcoal grill, grill kabobs on the greased grill rack of an uncovered grill directly over medium coals for 18 to 20 minutes or until pork is no longer pink and juices run clear, turning once halfway through grilling and brushing with the oil mixture during the last 4 minutes of grilling. (For a gas grill, preheat grill. Reduce heat to medium. Place kabobs on grill rack over heat. Cover and grill as above.)

4 Just before serving, sprinkle kabobs with Parmesan cheese.

Nutrition Facts per serving: 354 cal., 23 g total fat (3 g sat. fat), 75 mg chol., 468 mg sodium, 5 g carbo., 1 g fiber, 32 g pro.

ham steaks WITH FRESH PEACH CHUTNEY

To bring out the natural sweetness of ham steaks and to keep them juicy during grilling, glaze them with orange juice and tequila.

Prep: 20 minutes
Marinate: 10 minutes
Grill: 8 minutes
Makes: 6 servings

- 1 pound ripe peaches, peeled and chopped, or nectarines, chopped
- ½ cup finely chopped peeled and seeded cucumber
- ½ cup orange juice
- ¼ cup finely chopped red onion
- 1 tablespoon finely snipped fresh mint
- 1 tablespoon tequila
- ¼ teaspoon salt
- ⅛ teaspoon ground black pepper
- ½ cup orange juice
- 2 tablespoons tequila
- 2 1- to 1¼-pound cooked ham steaks, cut ½ inch thick

1 For chutney, in a medium bowl combine peaches, cucumber, ½ cup orange juice, red onion, mint, the 1 tablespoon tequila, salt, and pepper. Set aside.

2 For marinade, in a shallow glass dish combine ½ cup orange juice and the 2 tablespoons tequila. Set aside ¼ cup of the orange juice mixture to serve with the grilled ham.

3 Add ham steaks to the remaining marinade in dish. Marinate at room temperature for 10 minutes, turning once. Remove ham from marinade, reserving marinade.

4 For a charcoal grill, grill ham on the rack of an uncovered grill directly over medium-hot coals about 8 minutes or until heated through (140°F), turning and brushing once with the reserved marinade halfway through grilling. (For a gas grill, preheat grill. Reduce heat to medium-high. Place ham on grill rack over heat. Cover and grill as above.) Discard any remaining marinade.

5 Cut ham into serving-size pieces. Transfer to a serving platter. Pour the reserved orange juice mixture over top of ham. Serve with chutney.

Nutrition Facts per serving: 251 cal., 7 g total fat (2 g sat. fat), 68 mg chol., 2,017 mg sodium, 12 g carbo., 1 g fiber, 31 g pro.

ribs

East–West Ribs, *recipe page 132*

apricot-habanero SHORT RIBS

Habanero peppers and their near-identical cousins, Scotch bonnets, are some of the hottest peppers grown. Those with more tender palates may opt to substitute jalapeño or orange sweet peppers.

Prep: 20 minutes
Cook: 1½ hours
Grill: 15 minutes
Makes: 6 servings

- 3 pounds beef short ribs
- ¼ cup chopped onion
- 3 cloves garlic, minced
- 1 tablespoon cooking oil
- ½ cup ketchup
- ½ cup apricot preserves
- ¼ cup cider vinegar
- 1 habanero or Scotch bonnet pepper, seeded, if desired, and finely chopped
- 1 tablespoon bottled steak sauce
- 1 teaspoon chili powder
- ½ teaspoon ground cumin
- ¼ teaspoon salt

1 Trim fat from ribs. Place ribs in a 4- to 6-quart pot with enough water to cover ribs. Bring to boiling; reduce heat. Simmer, covered, for 1½ hours or until tender. Drain.

2 For sauce, in a small saucepan cook onion and garlic in hot oil until tender. Stir in ketchup, preserves, vinegar, pepper, steak sauce, and chili powder. Bring to boiling; reduce heat. Simmer, uncovered, about 10 minutes or until mixture thickens slightly, stirring occasionally. Set aside.

3 In a small bowl stir together cumin and salt. Sprinkle mixture evenly over both sides of ribs; rub into meat.

4 For a charcoal grill, arrange medium-hot coals around a drip pan. Test for medium heat above the pan. Place ribs, bone sides down, on lightly oiled grill rack directly over drip pan. Cover; grill for 15 minutes or until ribs are tender, brushing occasionally with sauce. (For a gas grill, preheat grill. Reduce heat to medium. Adjust grill for indirect cooking. Grill as above.) Heat remaining sauce until bubbly; pass with ribs.

Nutrition Facts per serving: 284 cal., 11 g total fat (4 g sat. fat), 44 mg chol., 444 mg sodium, 26 g carbo., 1 g fiber, 19 g pro.

k.c.-style BEEF RIBS

In Kansas City's renowned barbecue joints, pork is more common than beef. But these succulent beef ribs are proof that K.C. chefs know their way around both kinds of meat.

Prep: 25 minutes
Marinate: 4 to 24 hours
Grill: 1¼ hours
Makes: 6 to 8 servings

- ½ cup cider vinegar
- 3 tablespoons sugar
- 2 teaspoons dry mustard
- ⅛ teaspoon salt
- 2 cups pineapple juice
- ½ cup Worcestershire sauce
- ⅓ cup chopped onion (1 small)
- 2 tablespoons cooking oil
- 2½ to 3 pounds boneless beef short ribs
- 4 teaspoons paprika
- 1½ teaspoons sugar
- 1 teaspoon garlic powder
- ½ teaspoon pepper
- ¼ teaspoon salt
- 4 cups wood chips or 10 to 12 wood chunks (hickory or oak)

1 For marinade, in a medium saucepan bring vinegar to boiling. Remove from heat. Stir in the 3 tablespoons sugar, the dry mustard, and the ⅛ teaspoon salt. Stir until sugar is dissolved. Stir in pineapple juice, Worcestershire sauce, onion, and oil. Cool to room temperature.

2 Trim fat from ribs. Cut ribs into serving-size pieces. Place ribs in a large resealable plastic bag set in a shallow dish. Pour marinade over ribs; seal bag. Marinate in the refrigerator for 4 to 24 hours, turning bag occasionally.

3 Meanwhile, for rub, in a small bowl stir together paprika, the 1½ teaspoons sugar, the garlic powder, pepper, and the ¼ teaspoon salt; set aside.

4 At least 1 hour before grilling, soak wood chips in enough water to cover.

5 Drain ribs, discarding marinade. Pat dry with paper towels. Generously sprinkle rub over both sides of ribs; rub in with your fingers.

6 Drain wood chips. For a charcoal grill, arrange medium-hot coals around a drip pan. Test for medium heat above pan. Sprinkle one-fourth of the wood chips over the coals. Place ribs on grill rack over drip pan. Cover; grill for 1¼ to 1½ hours or until tender. Add more wood chips every 15 minutes and add more coals as necessary. (For a gas grill, preheat grill. Reduce heat to medium. Adjust grill for indirect cooking. Add wood chips according to manufacturer's directions. Grill as above, except place ribs, fat sides up, in a roasting pan.)

Nutrition Facts per serving: 770 cal., 69 g total fat (30 g sat. fat), 144 mg chol., 231 mg sodium, 7 g carbo., 0 g fiber, 28 g pro.

lone STAR BBQ RIBS

The flavor of the beer come through the marinade, so be sure to use one of your favorites. Be careful: Although the sauce might not seem hot at first, it'll sneak up on you!

Prep: 25 minutes
Marinate: 4 to 24 hours
Cook: 1 hour
Grill: 10 minutes
Makes: 4 to 5 servings

- 4 to 5 pounds beef back ribs
- 3 12-ounce bottles or cans bock beer or dark beer
- 2 cups water
- 2 bay leaves
- 4 medium onions, sliced (2 cups)
- ¼ cup butter or margarine
- ¼ cup packed brown sugar
- 2 cups ketchup
- ½ cup canned chipotle peppers in adobo sauce
- ¼ cup Worcestershire sauce
- ¼ cup lemon juice
- ¼ cup bottled hoisin sauce
- ¼ cup balsamic vinegar

1 Trim fat from ribs. Cut ribs into 2 portions. Place ribs in a 4-quart stainless-steel Dutch oven or a very large bowl. Pour beer over ribs. Cover and marinate in the refrigerator for 4 to 24 hours.

2 If necessary, transfer ribs and beer to a Dutch oven. Add the water and bay leaves. Bring to boiling; reduce heat. Simmer, covered, for 1 hour.

3 Meanwhile, in a large saucepan cook onions in butter over medium heat about 12 minutes or until tender. Stir in brown sugar; cook for 2 minutes more. Remove half of the onion mixture; set aside. For sauce, stir ketchup, chipotle peppers in adobo sauce, Worcestershire sauce, lemon juice, hoisin sauce, and vinegar into remaining onion mixture. Bring to boiling; reduce heat to medium-low. Simmer, uncovered, for 40 minutes, stirring occasionally. Remove from heat. Cool slightly. In a food processor or blender process or blend catsup mixture, half at a time, until smooth. Strain through a fine-mesh strainer, discarding solids; set sauce aside.

4 Drain ribs, discarding liquid and bay leaves. Brush ribs with some of the sauce. For a charcoal grill, grill ribs, bone sides down, on the rack of an uncovered grill directly over medium coals about 10 minutes or until browned. (For a gas grill, preheat grill. Reduce heat to medium. Place ribs on grill rack over heat. Cover and grill as above.)

5 To serve, reheat remaining sauce until bubbly. Serve ribs with warm sauce and reserved onion mixture.

Nutrition Facts per serving: 719 cal., 21 g total fat (10 g sat. fat), 185 mg chol., 2324 mg sodium, 72 g carbo., 5 g fiber, 58 g pro.

thai-coconut RIBS

These grilled ribs marinate in a spicy and gingery coconut-milk sauce that will send your taste buds to Thailand.

Prep: 15 minutes
Marinate: 8 to 24 hours
Grill: 1¼ hours
Makes: 6 servings

- 4 pounds pork loin back ribs
- 1 cup coconut milk
- 3 tablespoons brown sugar
- 3 tablespoons soy sauce
- 1 tablespoon grated fresh ginger
- 1 teaspoon finely shredded lime peel
- 1 tablespoon lime juice
- 4 cloves garlic, minced
- 1 teaspoon crushed red pepper

1 Trim fat from ribs. Cut ribs into 6 serving-size pieces. Place ribs in a resealable plastic bag set in a shallow dish. For marinade, in a small bowl combine coconut milk, brown sugar, soy sauce, ginger, lime peel, lime juice, garlic, and red pepper. Pour over ribs; seal bag. Marinate in the refrigerator for 8 to 24 hours, turning bag occasionally. Drain ribs, reserving marinade.

2 For a charcoal grill, arrange medium-hot coals around a drip pan. Test for medium heat above the pan. Place ribs, bone sides down, on grill rack over drip pan. Cover and grill for 1¼ to 1½ hours or until ribs are tender, brushing frequently with marinade during the first hour of grilling. Discard marinade. For a gas grill, preheat grill. Reduce heat to medium. Adjust for indirect cooking. Grill as above, except place the ribs in a roasting pan.

Nutrition Facts per serving: 431 cal., 32 g total fat (16 g sat. fat), 99 mg chol., 607 mg sodium, 9 g carbo., 0 g fiber, 25 g pro.

reggae BABY BACK RIBS

Prep: 30 minutes
Marinate: 8 to 24 hours
Grill: 1½ hours
Makes: 4 large servings

- ¼ cup packed brown sugar
- 2 tablespoons grated fresh ginger
- 2 teaspoons salt
- 2 teaspoons finely shredded lime peel
- 1 teaspoon ground cumin
- ½ teaspoon ground cinnamon
- 4 pounds pork loin back ribs, cut into 6- to 8-rib portions
- ½ cup chicken broth
- ¼ cup dark rum
- 3 tablespoons lime juice
- 1 tablespoon cooking oil or olive oil
- 1 small fresh habanero chile pepper, finely chopped**
- Mango-Guava BBQ Sauce*

1 In a small bowl combine brown sugar, ginger, salt, lime peel, cumin, and cinnamon. Sprinkle mixture evenly over ribs; rub in with your fingers. Place ribs in a resealable plastic bag; seal bag. Marinate in the refrigerator for 8 to 24 hours.

2 For mop sauce, in a medium bowl combine broth, rum, lime juice, oil, and habanero pepper. Cover and chill for 8 to 24 hours.

3 For a charcoal grill, arrange medium-hot coals around a drip pan in a grill with a cover. Test for medium heat above pan. Place ribs, bone sides down, on the grill rack over pan. Cover and grill for 1½ to 1¾ hours or until ribs are tender, brushing with mop sauce every 15 to 20 minutes. (For a gas grill, preheat grill. Reduce heat to medium. Adjust for indirect cooking. Cover and grill as above, except place ribs in a roasting pan.)

4 While ribs are cooking, prepare Mango-Guava BBQ Sauce. About 15 minutes before ribs are done, brush some of the mango sauce over ribs. Pass the remaining sauce.

***Mango-Guava BBQ Sauce:** In a small saucepan, combine 1⅓ cups chopped mangoes; ⅔ cup packed brown sugar; ⅔ cup chopped onion; ⅓ cup lime juice; ¼ cup olive oil; ¼ cup guava paste; 3 tablespoons honey; 2 tablespoons tomato paste; 2 cloves garlic, minced; and ¾ teaspoon ground cumin. Bring to boiling; reduce heat. Cover and simmer for 15 minutes. Cool slightly. Transfer to a food processor or blender. Cover and process or blend until slightly chunky.

Nutrition Facts per serving: 1,348 cal., 84 g total fat (27 g sat. fat), 228 mg chol., 1,585 mg sodium, 95 g carbo., 4 g fiber, 47 g pro.

****Note:** Because chile peppers contain volatile oils that can burn your skin and eyes, avoid direct contact with them as much as possible. When working with chile peppers, wear plastic or rubber gloves. If your bare hands do touch the peppers, wash your hands and nails well with soap and warm water.

chuck wagon BABY BACK RIBS

This recipe uses a unique grilling technique in which the sauce-smothered ribs braise inside the grill in an open roasting pan. To keep the roasting pan from blackening, wrap the outside with heavy foil.

Prep: 20 minutes
Grill: 1½ hours
Makes: 4 to 5 servings

- 4 to 5 pounds pork loin back ribs or meaty pork spareribs
- Chuck Wagon Rub*
- 1 cup dry red wine
- 1 cup pineapple juice
- ½ cup honey
- ½ cup cider vinegar
- ½ cup soy sauce
- ¼ cup yellow mustard
- 2 tablespoons bourbon
- 1 teaspoon bottled hot pepper sauce

1 Trim fat from ribs. Sprinkle Chuck Wagon Rub evenly over both sides of ribs; rub in with your fingers. If desired, cut ribs into 2- to 3-rib portions.

2 For sauce, in a large bowl combine wine, pineapple juice, honey, vinegar, soy sauce, mustard, bourbon, and hot pepper sauce.

3 Place rib portions, bone sides down, in a large roasting pan. Pour sauce over ribs. For a charcoal grill, arrange medium-hot coals around the edge of the grill. Test for medium heat above center of grill. Place uncovered roasting pan on grill rack in center of grill. Cover; grill for 1½ to 1¾ hours or until ribs are tender, spooning sauce over ribs every 20 to 25 minutes. (For a gas grill, preheat grill. Reduce heat to medium. Adjust for indirect cooking, except do not use a drip pan. Place uncovered roasting pan on grill rack directly over where drip pan would be. Grill as above.)

*Chuck Wagon Rub: In a small bowl combine 1 tablespoon black pepper, 2 teaspoons kosher salt or sea salt, 2 teaspoons chili powder, 1 teaspoon sugar, 1 teaspoon onion powder, 1 teaspoon garlic powder, 1 teaspoon dried parsley, and 1 teaspoon dried oregano, crushed.

Nutrition Facts per serving: 731 cal., 21 g total fat (7 g sat. fat), 135 mg chol., 3106 mg sodium, 52 g carbo., 2 g fiber, 68 g pro.

east–west RIBS

This recipe offers another angle on East meets West. The hoisin, ginger, and sesame flavors shine through.

Prep: 25 minutes
Marinate: 6 to 24 hours
Grill: 1½ hours
Makes: 4 to 5 servings

4 **pounds pork loin back ribs or meaty pork spareribs**
Hoisin-Ginger Glaze*
2 **cups hickory or apple wood chips**

❶ Trim fat from ribs. Place ribs in a resealable plastic bag set in a shallow dish. Cover and chill ½ cup of the Hoisin-Ginger Glaze. Pour the remaining glaze over the ribs; seal bag. Marinate in refrigerator for 6 hours to 24 hours, turning bag occasionally.

❷ At least 1 hour before grilling, soak wood chips in enough water to cover.

❸ Drain ribs, discarding marinade. Drain wood chips. For a charcoal grill, arrange medium-hot coals around a drip pan. Test for medium heat above pan. Sprinkle drained wood chips over coals. Place ribs, bone sides down, on grill rack over drip pan. (Or place ribs in a rib rack; place on the grill rack.) Cover; grill for 1½ to 1¾ hours or until ribs are tender, brushing occasionally with the ½ cup reserved glaze during the last 15 minutes of grilling. (For a gas grill, preheat grill. Reduce heat to medium. Adjust for indirect cooking. Grill as above, except place ribs in a roasting pan. Add wood chips according to manufacturer's directions.)

***Hoisin-Ginger Glaze:** In a medium bowl combine ½ cup hoisin sauce, ¼ cup bottled plum sauce, ¼ cup reduced-sodium soy sauce, 2 tablespoons dry sherry, 2 tablespoons toasted sesame oil, 2 tablespoons honey, 1 tablespoon grated fresh ginger, ½ teaspoon freshly ground black pepper, and 5 cloves garlic, minced.

Nutrition Facts per serving: 657 cal., 28 g total fat (8 g sat. fat), 135 mg chol., 1,179 mg sodium, 28 g carbo., 0 g fiber, 65 g pro.

chutney SPARERIBS

Serve these chutney barbecue sauce-glazed ribs with potato salad and grilled corn on the cob.

Prep: 35 minutes
Cook: 1 hour
Grill: 15 minutes
Makes: 6 servings

- 3 to 4 pounds meaty pork spareribs or loin back ribs
- Salt
- 1 cup mango chutney
- ¼ cup bottled chili sauce
- 2 tablespoons vinegar
- 1 tablespoon Worcestershire sauce
- 1 teaspoon dry mustard
- ½ teaspoon onion powder
- Several dashes bottled hot pepper sauce
- Fresh thyme sprigs (optional)

1 Cut ribs into serving-size pieces. Place ribs in a large pot. Add enough water to cover ribs. Bring to boiling; reduce heat. Cover and simmer about 1 hour or until meat is tender. Drain ribs; sprinkle lightly with salt.

2 Meanwhile, chop any large pieces of chutney. In a medium saucepan combine the chutney with the chili sauce, vinegar, Worcestershire sauce, 1 tablespoon water, dry mustard, onion powder, and hot pepper sauce. Cook and stir over medium heat until heated through.

3 Place ribs, meaty sides down, on rack of an uncovered grill directly over medium coals. Grill 10 minutes. Turn ribs meaty sides up; brush with some of the chutney sauce. Grill 5 minutes more. Pass remaining warmed chutney sauce. Garnish ribs with fresh thyme sprigs, if desired.

Nutrition Facts per serving: 421 cal., 23 g total fat (9 g sat. fat), 70 mg chol., 297 mg sodium, 29 g carbo., 1 g fiber, 23 g pro.

glazed COUNTRY RIBS

To prevent the rich, tart-sweet sauce from scorching before the ribs are done, brush it on only during the last 10 minutes of grilling.

Prep: 15 minutes
Cook: 10 minutes
Grill: 1½ hours
Makes: 4 servings

- 1 cup ketchup
- ½ cup water
- ¼ cup finely chopped onion
- ¼ cup cider vinegar or wine vinegar
- ¼ cup mild-flavor molasses
- 2 tablespoons Worcestershire sauce
- 2 teaspoons chili powder
- 2 cloves garlic, minced
- 2½ to 3 pounds pork country-style ribs

1 For sauce, in a medium saucepan combine ketchup, water, onion, vinegar, molasses, Worcestershire sauce, chili powder, and garlic. Bring to boiling; reduce heat. Simmer, uncovered, for 10 to 15 minutes or to desired consistency, stirring often.

2 Trim fat from ribs. For a charcoal grill, arrange medium-hot coals around a drip pan. Test for medium heat above pan. Place ribs, bone sides down, on grill rack over pan. (Or place ribs in a rib rack; place on grill rack.) Cover; grill for 1½ to 2 hours or until ribs are tender, brushing occasionally with sauce during the last 10 minutes of grilling. (For a gas grill, preheat grill. Reduce heat to medium. Adjust for indirect cooking. Grill as above, except place ribs in a roasting pan.) Pass remaining sauce with ribs.

Nutrition Facts per serving: 431 cal., 18 g total fat (6 g sat. fat), 112 mg chol., 852 mg sodium, 34 g carbo., 1 g fiber, 33 g pro.

mustard-glazed RIBS

Use this sassy glaze on spareribs or beef short ribs too. If an earthier flavor is what you're looking for, substitute sage for the savory.

Prep: 25 minutes
Grill: 1½ hours
Makes: 4 servings

- 2 tablespoons cooking oil
- ⅓ cup chopped sweet onion
- 1 cup whole grain, spicy brown, or other mustard
- 2 tablespoons honey
- 2 tablespoons cider vinegar
- 1 teaspoon snipped fresh summer savory or ⅛ teaspoon dried summer savory, crushed
- 3 pounds pork country-style ribs
- Orange slices (optional)

1 For glaze, in a medium saucepan heat oil over medium-high heat. Add onion and cook until golden brown. Reduce heat to low; stir in mustard, honey, and vinegar. Simmer for 3 minutes. Stir in savory; cook and stir for 1 minute more. Set aside, reserving about one-third of glaze to serve with ribs.

2 Trim excess fat from ribs. For a charcoal grill, arrange medium-hot coals around a drip pan. Test for medium heat above the pan. Place ribs, bone sides down, on lightly oiled grill rack directly over drip pan. Cover and grill for 1½ to 2 hours or until tender, brushing occasionally with glaze during the last 10 minutes of grilling. (For a gas grill, preheat grill. Reduce heat to medium. Adjust grill for indirect cooking. Grill as above.)

3 Heat and pass reserved glaze with ribs. Garnish with fresh orange slices, if desired.

Nutrition Facts per serving: 396 cal., 23 g total fat (5 g sat. fat), 101 mg chol., 904 mg sodium, 13 g carbo., 1 g fiber, 34 g pro.

beef

Three-Herb Steaks, *recipe page 147*

spanish MEAT LOAVES

Serve these diminutive, green olive-stuffed loaves with Barcelona-style Spanish rice or thinly sliced potatoes and onions cooked in a foil pack alongside them on the grill.

Prep: 15 minutes
Grill: 18 minutes
Makes: 4 servings

- 1 slightly beaten egg
- ¾ cup quick-cooking rolled oats
- ½ cup pimiento-stuffed green olives, sliced
- ¼ cup snipped fresh parsley
- ¼ cup tomato paste
- ¼ teaspoon pepper
- 1 pound lean ground beef
- ¼ cup jalapeño pepper jelly or apple jelly, melted
- 1 medium tomato, chopped
- ⅓ cup chunky salsa
- ¼ cup chopped, seeded cucumber
- 2 tablespoons sliced pimiento-stuffed green olives (optional)

1 In a medium bowl combine egg, rolled oats, the ½ cup olives, the parsley, tomato paste, and pepper. Add ground beef; mix well. Shape into four 4x2½x1-inch meat loaves.

2 For a charcoal grill, grill meat loaves on the rack of an uncovered grill directly over medium coals for 16 to 18 minutes or until meat is no longer pink, turning once halfway through grilling. Brush with melted jelly; grill for 2 minutes more. (For a gas grill, preheat grill. Reduce heat to medium. Place meat loaves on grill rack over heat. Cover and grill as above.)

3 Meanwhile, for relish, in a small bowl combine the tomato, salsa, cucumber, and, if desired, the 2 tablespoons olives. Serve the meat loaves with relish.

Nutrition Facts per serving: 362 cal., 16 g total fat (5 g sat. fat), 125 mg chol., 479 mg sodium, 31 g carbo., 2 g fiber, 26 g pro.

ribeyes WITH AVOCADO SAUCE

Ribeye is one of the most tender and flavorful steaks you can buy. Its partner, the rib steak, is basically the same cut with the addition of a large, curved bone on the side. Both steaks taste great grilled.

Prep: 25 minutes
Marinate: 30 minutes
Grill: 15 minutes
Makes: 4 to 6 servings

- 2 12-ounce boneless beef ribeye or top loin steaks, cut 1¼ to 1½ inches thick
- 1 tablespoon packed brown sugar
- 1 teaspoon chili powder
- ½ teaspoon garlic salt
- ½ teaspoon black pepper
- 8 ounces fresh tomatillos, husked and quartered (6 medium)
- ¼ cup water
- 2 ounces cream cheese
- 1 avocado, halved, seeded, peeled, and cut up
- ¼ cup sliced green onions (2)
- ½ teaspoon salt
- 1 medium red onion, sliced ½ inch thick
- 1 teaspoon cooking oil

1 Trim fat from steaks. For rub, in a small bowl combine brown sugar, chili powder, garlic salt, and pepper. Sprinkle rub evenly over both sides of the steaks; rub in with your fingers. Cover and chill for 30 minutes.

2 Meanwhile, for sauce, in a small saucepan bring tomatillos and water to boiling; reduce heat. Cover and simmer for 5 to 7 minutes or until tomatillos are soft. Drain. Stir in cream cheese until melted; cool mixture slightly. In a food processor or blender combine tomatillo mixture, avocado, sliced green onions, and salt; cover and process or blend until smooth. Transfer sauce to a serving bowl.

3 For a charcoal grill, grill steaks on rack of an uncovered grill directly over medium coals until desired doneness, turning once halfway through grilling. Allow 15 to 19 minutes for medium-rare (145°F) or 18 to 23 minutes for medium doneness (160°F). Brush the onion slices lightly with oil. Grill directly over medium heat about 5 minutes, turning occasionally. (For a gas grill, preheat grill. Reduce heat to medium. Place steaks, then onion slices on grill rack over heat. Cover and grill as above.)

4 To serve, slice steaks. Serve with sauce and grilled onions.

Nutrition Facts per serving: 425 cal., 24 g total fat (8 g sat. fat), 96 mg chol., 556 mg sodium, 13 g carbo., 4 g fiber, 40 g pro.

roasted GARLIC STEAK

Roasting the garlic with herbs results in a delicious, mild garlic flavor that brings out the best in beef.

Prep: 15 minutes
Grill: 30 minutes
Makes: 6 servings

- 1 or 2 whole garlic bulb(s)
- 3 to 4 teaspoons snipped fresh basil or 1 teaspoon dried basil, crushed
- 1 tablespoon snipped fresh rosemary or 1 teaspoon dried rosemary, crushed
- 2 tablespoons olive oil or cooking oil
- 1½ pounds boneless beef ribeye steaks or sirloin steak, cut 1 inch thick
- 1 to 2 teaspoons cracked black pepper
- ½ teaspoon salt

1 With a sharp knife, cut off the top ½ inch from each garlic bulb to expose the ends of the individual cloves. Leaving garlic bulb(s) whole, remove any loose, papery outer layers.

2 Fold a 20x18-inch piece of heavy foil in half crosswise. Trim into a 10-inch square. Place garlic bulb(s), cut sides up, in center of foil square. Sprinkle garlic with basil and rosemary and drizzle with oil. Bring up opposite edges of foil and seal with a double fold. Fold remaining edges together to completely enclose garlic, leaving space for steam to build.

3 For a charcoal grill, grill garlic on the rack of an uncovered grill directly over medium coals about 30 minutes or until garlic feels soft when packet is squeezed, turning garlic occasionally.

4 Meanwhile, trim fat from steaks. Sprinkle pepper and salt evenly over both sides of steaks; rub in with your fingers. While garlic is grilling, add steaks to grill. Grill to desired doneness, turning once halfway through grilling. For ribeye steaks, allow 10 to 12 minutes for medium-rare (145°F) and 12 to 15 minutes for medium doneness (160°F). For sirloin steak, allow 14 to 18 minutes for medium-rare (145°F) and 18 to 22 minutes for medium doneness (160°F). (For a gas grill, preheat grill. Reduce heat to medium. Place garlic, then steaks on grill rack over heat. Cover and grill as above.)

5 To serve, cut steaks into 6 serving-size pieces. Remove garlic from foil, reserving oil mixture. Squeeze garlic pulp from each clove onto steaks. Mash pulp slightly with a fork; spread over steaks. Drizzle with reserved oil mixture.

Nutrition Facts per serving: 189 cal., 9 g total fat (2 g sat. fat), 52 mg chol., 139 mg sodium, 4 g carbo., 0 g fiber, 22 g pro.

ribeye steaks WITH HOT-AS-HECK SAUCE

These sizzling ribeye steaks fire up your palate with a hot and smoky chipotle pepper sauce.

Prep: 10 minutes
Cook: 20 minutes
Grill: 10 minutes
Makes: 4 servings

- ⅓ cup sugar
- ½ cup finely chopped onion (1 medium)
- 2 cloves garlic, minced
- 1½ cups light beer or water
- 1 6-ounce can tomato paste
- ¼ cup Worcestershire sauce
- ¼ cup vinegar
- 1 to 2 tablespoons bottled habanero hot pepper sauce
- 1 tablespoon chopped canned chipotle peppers in adobo sauce
- Salt
- 4 beef ribeye or sirloin strip steaks, cut 1 inch thick

1 For sauce, in a medium saucepan cook sugar over medium-high heat until it begins to melt, shaking the pan occasionally (do not stir). Reduce heat to low; add onion and garlic. Cook and stir for 5 minutes more or until mixture is golden brown. Bring beer just to boiling in a small skillet. Carefully and gradually add boiling beer to sugar mixture, stirring constantly. Whisk in tomato paste, Worcestershire sauce, vinegar, habanero sauce, chipotle peppers, and salt. Bring to boiling; reduce heat. Simmer, uncovered, for 15 to 20 minutes or to desired consistency. Set aside.

2 For a charcoal grill, grill steaks on the rack of an uncovered grill directly over medium coals until desired doneness, turning once and brushing with some of the sauce during the last few minutes of grilling. Allow 10 to 12 minutes for medium-rare (145°F) or 12 to 15 minutes for medium doneness (160°F). (For a gas grill, preheat grill. Reduce heat to medium. Place steaks on grill rack over heat. Cover and grill as above.)

3 Pass remaining sauce with steaks. Cover and chill any remaining sauce for up to 1 week.

Nutrition Facts per serving: 572 cal., 18 g total fat (7 g sat. fat), 134 mg chol., 532 mg sodium, 31 g carbo., 2 g fiber, 65 g pro.

porterhouse STEAK WITH CHIPOTLE POTATO HASH

Because of its marbling and tenderness, porterhouse is considered a premium cut. Treat it to a simple rub and serve with spicy potato hash for a main dish that turns weekend cookouts into special occasions.

Prep: 30 minutes
Cook: 9 minutes
Grill: 15 minutes
Makes: 2 to 3 servings

- 1   1½-pound beef porterhouse steak, cut 1½ inches thick
- ¼   teaspoon ground chipotle chile pepper
- ⅛   teaspoon garlic salt
- ⅛   teaspoon black pepper
- 1   medium russet potato, peeled and finely chopped (1¼ cups)
- ¼   cup finely chopped sweet onion
- 1   tablespoon olive oil or cooking oil
- 1   teaspoon chili powder
- ½   teaspoon dried marjoram or dried oregano, crushed
- ¼   teaspoon salt
- ⅓   cup tomato juice
- 1   tablespoon snipped fresh cilantro

1 Trim fat from steak. For rub, in a small bowl combine ⅛ teaspoon of the ground chipotle pepper, the garlic salt, and black pepper. Sprinkle evenly over both sides of steak; rub into meat with your fingers.

2 For a charcoal grill, grill steak on the rack of an uncovered grill directly over medium coals until desired doneness, turning once. Allow 15 to 18 minutes for medium-rare (145°F) or 18 to 21 minutes for medium doneness (160°F). (For a gas grill, preheat grill. Reduce heat to medium. Place meat on rack over heat. Cover and grill as above.)

3 Meanwhile, in a large skillet cook and stir potato and onion in hot oil over medium heat for 7 minutes or until tender. Stir in remaining ground chipotle pepper, chili powder, marjoram, and salt. Cook and stir for 1 minute. Remove from heat. Add tomato juice; return to heat and bring to boiling. Reduce heat and simmer, uncovered, about 1 minute or until most of the liquid evaporates. Stir in cilantro. To serve, spoon mixture over steak.

Nutrition Facts per serving: 497 cal., 24 g total fat (7 g sat. fat), 134 mg chol., 626 mg sodium, 21 g carbo., 2 g fiber, 48 g pro.

blt STEAK

A loaf of crusty bread and a bottle of red wine complete this bistro-style dinner.

Start to Finish: 30 minutes
Makes: 4 servings

- 2 boneless beef top loin steaks, cut 1¼ inches thick
- 2 slices bacon
- ½ cup bottled balsamic vinaigrette salad dressing
- 8 slices red and/or yellow tomato
- 2 cups mixed baby salad greens

1 Trim fat from steaks. For a charcoal grill, grill steaks on the rack of an uncovered grill directly over medium coals until desired doneness, turning once halfway through grilling. Allow 13 to 17 minutes for medium-rare (145°F) or 17 to 21 minutes for medium doneness (160°F). (For a gas grill, preheat grill. Reduce heat to medium. Place steaks on grill rack over heat. Cover and grill as above.)

2 Meanwhile, in a large skillet cook bacon over medium heat until crisp. Remove bacon and drain on paper towels. Crumble bacon and set aside. Drain fat, reserving 1 tablespoon drippings in skillet. Add the salad dressing to the skillet. Cook and stir over high heat about 1 minute, scraping up browned bits. Remove from heat.

3 To serve, halve the steaks. Place a piece of steak on each of four dinner plates. Top each with 2 tomato slices, some cooked bacon, some mixed greens, and a splash of dressing from the skillet.

Nutrition Facts per serving: 556 cal., 42 g total fat (14 g sat. fat), 122 mg chol., 636 mg sodium, 5 g carbo., 1 g fiber, 38 g pro.

three-herb STEAKS

Prep: 20 minutes
Chill: 1 hour
Grill: 15 minutes
Stand: 10 minutes
Makes: 6 servings

- ½ cup snipped fresh parsley
- ¼ cup olive oil
- ¼ cup snipped fresh basil
- 1 tablespoon snipped fresh oregano
- 1 to 2 tablespoons cracked black pepper
- ½ teaspoon salt
- 2 beef top loin steaks, cut 1½ inches thick
- 2 medium red or yellow sweet peppers, cut into ½-inch rings, seeds removed
- 1 tablespoon olive oil
- Salt
- Ground black pepper

1 For rub, in a small bowl combine parsley, ¼ cup olive oil, basil, oregano, cracked black pepper, and ½ teaspoon salt. Trim fat from meat. Sprinkle half the mixture on both sides of each steak; rub in with your fingers. Cover and chill steaks for 1 hour. Meanwhile, brush pepper rings with 1 tablespoon olive oil. Season lightly with salt and black pepper.

2 For a charcoal grill, place steaks on the grill rack directly over medium coals. Grill, uncovered, until steaks reach desired doneness, turning once. (Allow 15 to 19 minutes for medium-rare (145°F) or 18 to 23 minutes for medium (160°F). Grill pepper rings next to the steaks the last 8 to 10 minutes of grilling, or until peppers are tender, turning once. (For a gas grill, preheat grill. Reduce heat to medium. Place steaks on grill rack over heat. Cover and grill steaks and peppers as above.) Remove steaks from grill and sprinkle with remaining herb mixture. Cover and let stand for 10 minutes.

3 To serve, slice steaks across the grain. Serve with sweet pepper rings.

Nutrition Facts per serving: 307 cal., 19 g total fat (5 g sat. fat), 77 mg chol., 313 mg sodium, 3 g carbo., 1 g fiber, 29 g pro.

flat-iron steak WITH BALSAMIC TOMATOES

In some regions flat-iron steaks are called beef shoulder top blade steaks. By either name they're a good value, providing tender, juicy eating at a modest price.

Prep: 10 minutes
Marinate: 2 to 24 hours
Grill: 7 minutes
Makes: 6 servings

Balsamic Tomatoes*
- 1 tablespoon dried marjoram, crushed
- ½ teaspoon garlic salt
- ½ teaspoon freshly ground black pepper
- 4 beef shoulder top blade (flat-iron) steaks, cut ¾ inch thick
- Arugula (optional)

1 Prepare Balsamic Tomatoes. For rub, in a small bowl combine marjoram, garlic salt, and pepper. Sprinkle rub evenly over both sides of steaks; rub in with your fingers. If desired, cover and chill for 2 to 24 hours.

2 For a charcoal grill, grill steaks on the rack of an uncovered grill directly over medium coals until desired doneness, turning once halfway through grilling. Allow 7 to 9 minutes for medium-rare (145°F) or 10 to 12 minutes for medium doneness (160°F). (For a gas grill, preheat grill. Reduce heat to medium. Place steaks on grill rack over heat. Cover and grill as above.)

3 Serve steaks with Balsamic Tomatoes and, if desired, arugula. If desired, drizzle with marinade from Balsamic Tomatoes.

***Balsamic Tomatoes:** Remove the core from 2 ripe medium tomatoes. Trim off ends. Cut tomatoes crosswise into ¾-inch slices. Arrange tomato slices in a shallow dish; sprinkle lightly with salt and pepper. Pour ⅓ cup balsamic vinegar over tomatoes. Drizzle with 3 tablespoons olive oil. Cover and chill for 2 to 24 hours, turning occasionally. Remove tomatoes, reserving marinade. For a charcoal grill, grill tomatoes on the rack of an uncovered grill directly over medium coals for 4 minutes or until lightly charred and slightly soft, turning once. (For a gas grill, preheat grill. Reduce heat to medium. Place tomatoes on grill rack over heat. Cover and grill as above.)

Nutrition Facts per serving: 277 cal., 16 g total fat (4 g sat. fat), 69 mg chol., 273 mg sodium, 6 g carbo., 1 g fiber, 26 g pro.

sausage-and-pepper- SMOTHERED STEAK

Prep: 30 minutes
Chill: 1 hour
Grill: 17 minutes
Makes: 6 to 8 servings

- 1 2-pound beef flank steak
- Salt
- Freshly ground black pepper
- 2 teaspoons finely shredded lime peel
- 4 ounces bulk Italian sausage
- 1½ cups chopped onions (2 large)
- 1½ cups chopped red, yellow, and/or green sweet peppers (2 medium)
- 3 cloves garlic, minced
- ¼ cup snipped fresh cilantro
- ¼ cup cider vinegar

1 Trim fat from steak. Score both sides of steak in a diamond pattern, making shallow diagonal cuts at 1-inch intervals. Sprinkle steak with salt, black pepper, and lime peel. Wrap in plastic wrap and chill for 1 hour.

2 For a charcoal grill, place steak on the grill rack directly over medium coals. Grill, uncovered, for 17 to 21 minutes for medium doneness (160°F), turning once halfway through grilling. (For a gas grill, preheat grill. Reduce heat to medium. Place steak on the grill rack over heat. Cover and grill as above.)

3 Meanwhile, preheat a large cast-iron skillet next to steak directly over medium coals. Add sausage; cook, stirring occasionally, for 3 minutes. Add onions, sweet peppers, and garlic. Cook, stirring occasionally, for 8 to 10 minutes more or until vegetables are crisp-tender. Stir in cilantro and vinegar. Remove from heat.

4 To serve, thinly slice steak. Spoon pepper mixture on top of steak.

Nutrition Facts per serving: 351 cal., 19 g total fat (7 g sat. fat), 76 mg chol., 321 mg sodium, 8 g carbo., 2 g fiber, 36 g pro.

stuffed STEAK PINWHEELS

Overstuffed with spinach and bacon, these pinwheels are nice to look at and good to eat. (Just don't forget to take out the toothpicks.)

Prep: 20 minutes
Grill: 12 minutes
Makes: 4 servings

- 8 slices bacon
- 1 1 to 1½-pound beef flank steak or top round steak
- ¾ teaspoon lemon-pepper seasoning
- ¼ teaspoon salt
- 1 10-ounce package frozen chopped spinach, thawed and well drained
- 2 tablespoons fine dry bread crumbs
- ½ teaspoon dried thyme, crushed
- Dash salt

1 In a large skillet cook bacon over medium heat just until brown but not crisp. Remove from skillet; drain on paper towels. Set aside.

2 Trim fat from steak. Score both sides of steak by making shallow diagonal cuts at 1-inch intervals in a diamond pattern. Place steak between two pieces of plastic wrap. Working from center to the edges, use flat side of a meat mallet to pound steak into a 12x8-inch rectangle. Remove plastic wrap. Sprinkle with ½ teaspoon of the lemon-pepper seasoning and the ¼ teaspoon salt. Arrange bacon lengthwise on steak.

3 For filling, in a medium bowl combine spinach, bread crumbs, thyme, the remaining ¼ teaspoon lemon-pepper seasoning, and the dash salt. Spread over bacon. Starting from a short side, roll up. Secure with wooden toothpicks at 1-inch intervals, starting ½ inch from one end. Slice between toothpicks into eight 1-inch pinwheels. Thread 2 pinwheels onto each of four metal skewers.

4 For a charcoal grill, grill pinwheels on the rack of an uncovered grill directly over medium coals until desired doneness, turning once halfway through grilling. (Allow 12 to 14 minutes for medium doneness.) (For a gas grill, preheat grill. Reduce heat to medium. Place pinwheels on grill rack over heat. Cover and grill as above.) To serve, remove from skewers.

Nutrition Facts per serving: 265 cal., 15 g total fat (6 g sat. fat), 64 mg chol., 702 mg sodium, 5 g carbo., 2 g fiber, 27 g pro.

easy STEAK AND POTATO KABOBS

This is the perfect kabob for meat-and-potato lovers. The marinade, based on bottled salad dressing, is deliciously easy.

Prep: 20 minutes
Marinate: 4 to 6 hours
Grill: 12 minutes
Makes: 4 servings

- 1 boneless beef sirloin steak, cut 1 inch thick
- ¼ cup bottled red wine vinegar and oil salad dressing
- 2 tablespoons snipped fresh thyme or 2 teaspoons dried thyme, crushed
- 2 tablespoons Worcestershire sauce
- ¼ teaspoon garlic powder
- 2 medium green and/or yellow sweet peppers, cut into 1-inch squares
- 1 medium red onion, cut into wedges
- ½ of a 20-ounce package refrigerated potato wedges (about 32 wedges)

1 Trim fat from steak. Cut steak into 1-inch cubes. Place steak cubes in a resealable plastic bag set in a shallow dish. For marinade, in a bowl combine salad dressing, thyme, Worcestershire sauce, and garlic powder. Pour over steak; seal bag. Marinate in the refrigerator for 4 to 6 hours, turning bag occasionally.

2 Drain steak, reserving marinade. On eight 10-inch metal skewers, alternately thread steak, sweet peppers, onion, and potato wedges, leaving a ¼-inch space between pieces.

3 For a charcoal grill, grill kabobs on the rack of an uncovered grill directly over medium coals until meat is desired doneness, turning once and brushing occasionally with reserved marinade up to the last 5 minutes of grilling. (Allow 12 to 14 minutes for medium doneness (160°F).) (For a gas grill, preheat grill. Reduce heat to medium. Place kabobs on grill rack over heat. Cover and grill as above.) Discard any remaining marinade.

Nutrition Facts per serving: 230 cal., 5 g total fat (2 g sat. fat), 69 mg chol., 230 mg sodium, 17 g carbo., 4 g fiber, 27 g pro.

five-spice TRI-TIP ROAST WITH DAIKON RELISH

Five-spice powder, often used in Asian cooking, is slightly sweet and mildly spicy. You can find it at Asian markets and in the spice section at supermarkets.

Prep: 10 minutes
Marinate: 2 to 4 hours
Grill: 35 minutes
Stand: 15 minutes
Makes: 6 servings

- 1 1½- to 2-pound boneless beef tri-tip roast
- 1 tablespoon toasted sesame oil
- 2 teaspoons five-spice powder
- ½ teaspoon salt
- Daikon Relish*

1 Trim fat from meat. In a small bowl stir together sesame oil, five-spice powder, and salt. Place meat in a resealable plastic bag set in a shallow dish. Pour oil mixture over meat; seal bag. Marinate in the refrigerator for 2 to 4 hours, turning bag occasionally.

2 For a charcoal grill, arrange medium-hot coals around a drip pan. Test for medium heat above the pan. Place meat on grill rack over drip pan. Cover; grill until desired doneness. Allow 35 to 40 minutes for medium-rare (135°F) and 40 to 45 minutes for medium doneness (150°F). (For a gas grill, preheat grill. Reduce heat to medium. Adjust grill for indirect cooking. Grill as above except place meat on a rack in a roasting pan.) Remove meat from grill. Cover with foil; let stand for 15 minutes before slicing. (The meat's temperature will rise 10°F during standing.) Serve slices topped with Daikon Relish.

*****Daikon Relish:** Finely chop 8 ounces peeled daikon radish or jicama (you should have about 1¾ cups). In a medium bowl combine chopped daikon, ⅓ cup seasoned rice vinegar, 1 teaspoon crushed red pepper, and ½ teaspoon toasted sesame oil.

Nutrition Facts per serving: 196 cal., 8 g total fat (2 g sat. fat), 54 mg chol., 267 mg sodium, 3 g carbo., 1 g fiber, 26 g pro.

peppered RIB ROAST

A robust pepper-and-herb rub clings to the meat throughout grilling.

Prep: 10 minutes
Grill: 2¼ hours
Stand: 15 minutes
Makes: 10 to 12 servings

- 1 6-pound beef rib roast
- 4 teaspoons coarsely ground black pepper
- 2 tablespoons finely chopped shallots
- 1 teaspoon coarse salt
- 1 teaspoon dried basil, crushed
- 1 teaspoon dried thyme, crushed
- 1 tablespoon olive oil

1 Trim fat from meat. For rub, combine pepper, shallots, salt, basil, and thyme. Brush meat with oil. Rub pepper mixture over surface of roast with fingers. Insert a meat thermometer into center of meat without touching bone.

2 For a charcoal grill, arrange medium coals around drip pan. Test for medium-low heat above pan. Place roast, bone side down, on grill rack over drip pan. Cover; grill until meat thermometer registers desired doneness. Allow 2¼ to 2¾ hours for medium-rare (135°F) or 2¾ to 3¼ hours for medium doneness (150°F). (For a gas grill, preheat grill. Reduce heat to medium-low. Adjust grill for indirect cooking. Grill as above, except place meat on rack in a roasting pan.)

3 Remove meat from grill. Cover with foil and let stand for 15 minutes before carving. (The meat's temperature will rise 10°F during standing.)

Nutrition Facts per serving: 310 cal., 18 g total fat (7 g sat. fat), 100 mg chol., 305 mg sodium, 1 g carbo., 0 g fiber, 34 g pro.

raspberry-sesame TRI-TIP ROAST

Raspberry vinaigrette salad dressing does double duty as both marinade for the beef and dressing for the crisp slaw.

Prep: 25 minutes
Marinate: 2 to 4 hours
Grill: 35 minutes
Stand: 15 minutes
Makes: 6 servings

- 1 1½- to 2-pound boneless beef tri-tip roast
- 1¼ cups bottled raspberry vinaigrette salad dressing
- ¼ cup sesame seeds, toasted
- 3 cups shredded romaine
- 1 cup thinly sliced Belgian endive
- ½ of a small red onion, very thinly sliced

1 Trim fat from meat. Place meat in a resealable plastic bag set in a shallow dish. Pour 1 cup of the salad dressing over meat; seal bag. Marinate in the refrigerator for 2 to 4 hours, turning bag occasionally. Drain meat, discarding marinade. Coat meat with sesame seeds (some seeds will fall off during handling and grilling).

2 For a charcoal grill, arrange medium coals around a drip pan. Test for medium heat above pan. Place roast on lightly oiled grill rack over drip pan. Cover; grill until desired doneness. Allow 35 to 40 minutes for medium-rare (135°F) or 40 to 45 minutes for medium doneness (150°F). (For a gas grill, preheat grill. Reduce heat to medium. Adjust grill for indirect grilling. Grill as above except place meat in a roasting pan.)

3 Remove meat from grill. Cover with foil; let stand for 15 minutes before slicing. (The meat's temperature will rise 10°F during standing.)

4 Meanwhile, for slaw, in a medium bowl combine romaine, endive, and onion. Toss with remaining salad dressing. Cover and chill until ready to serve. Slice meat and serve with slaw.

Nutrition Facts per serving: 297 cal., 15 g total fat (2 g sat. fat), 54 mg chol., 616 mg sodium, 11 g carbo., 1 g fiber, 27 g pro.

fish
AND SEAFOOD

Sea Bass with Wilted Greens, recipe page 167

trout WITH MUSHROOM STUFFING

Prep: 25 minutes
Cook: 8 minutes
Grill: 20 minutes
Stand: 1 hour
Makes: 4 servings

1 cup apple or alder wood chips or chunks
4 10- to 12-ounce fresh or frozen pan-dressed trout
4 slices bacon, chopped
2 cups sliced assorted wild mushrooms (such as cremini, shiitake, chanterelle, oyster, porcini, and/or cepes)
3 tablespoons butter, melted
½ teaspoon salt
½ teaspoon coarsely ground black pepper
3 large cloves garlic, thinly sliced
8 sprigs fresh thyme
¼ cup dry white wine
Grilled Apple Slices* (optional)

1 At least 1 hour before grilling, soak wood chips or chunks and several wooden toothpicks in enough water to cover.

2 Thaw fish, if frozen. Rinse fish; pat dry with paper towels. For stuffing, in a large skillet cook bacon over medium heat for 3 to 4 minutes or until softened and beginning to brown. Add mushrooms; cook 5 to 8 minutes or until mushrooms are tender and most of the liquid has evaporated, stirring occasionally. Set aside.

3 Meanwhile, brush the outside and cavity of each fish with melted butter. For each fish, sprinkle cavity with salt, black pepper, and garlic slices. Add one-quarter of the mushroom mixture and 2 thyme sprigs. Sprinkle with 1 tablespoon wine. Secure stuffing inside fish with four to five short metal skewers or the soaked toothpicks. Place the fish on a sheet of heavy-duty foil.

4 Drain wood chips or chunks. For a charcoal grill, arrange medium-hot coals around a drip pan. Add drained wood chips or chunks to coals. Test for medium heat above the pan. Place foil with fish on grill rack over drip pan. Cover; grill for 20 to 25 minutes or until fish flakes easily when tested with a fork. For a gas grill, preheat grill. Reduce heat to medium. Add wood chips or chunks according to manufacturers directions. Adjust for indirect cooking. Grill as above.

5 If desired, serve with Grilled Apple Slices.

***Grilled Apple Slices:** Remove the core from 2 apples. Cut apples crosswise into ½-inch slices; brush with olive oil. Grill apple slices directly over medium heat for 5 to 6 minutes or until apples are tender, turning once. Serve warm with fish.

Nutrition Facts per serving: 544 cal., 29 g total fat (12 g sat. fat), 198 mg chol., 614 mg sodium, 3 g carbo., 1 g fiber, 63 g pro.

blackened SNAPPER WITH ROASTED POTATOES

This version of a southern favorite is served alongside tiny new potatoes, carrots, and onions roasted in olive oil and hot pepper sauce.

Prep: 20 minutes
Grill: 35 minutes
Makes: 4 servings

- 1 tablespoon olive oil
- ¼ teaspoon salt
- Several dashes bottled hot pepper sauce
- 1½ pounds tiny new potatoes, thinly sliced
- 4 medium carrots, thinly sliced
- 1 medium green sweet pepper, cut into thin strips
- 1 medium onion, sliced
- 4 4- to 5-ounce fresh or frozen red snapper or catfish fillets, ½ to 1 inch thick
- ½ teaspoon Cajun seasoning
- Nonstick cooking spray
- 1 tablespoon snipped fresh chervil or parsley

1 Tear a 48x18-inch piece of heavy-duty foil; fold in half to make a 24x18-inch rectangle. In a large bowl combine the oil, salt, and pepper sauce. Add the potatoes, carrots, sweet pepper, and onion; toss to coat. Place in the center of foil. Bring up two opposite edges of foil; seal with a double fold. Fold remaining ends to completely enclose vegetables, leaving space for steam to build.

2 For a charcoal grill, grill vegetables on the rack of an uncovered grill directly over medium coals for 35 to 40 minutes or until potatoes and carrots are tender. (For a gas grill, preheat grill. Reduce heat to medium. Place vegetables on grill rack over heat. Cover and grill as above.)

3 Meanwhile, thaw fish, if frozen. Rinse fish; pat dry with paper towels. Sprinkle both sides of fish evenly with Cajun seasoning and lightly coat with nonstick cooking spray. Place fish in a well-greased wire grill basket. Place grill basket on the grill rack next to the vegetables. For a charcoal grill, grill fish in basket on the rack of an uncovered grill directly over medium coals for 4 to 6 minutes per ½-inch thickness or until fish flakes easily when tested with a fork, turning the basket once. (For a gas grill, preheat grill. Reduce heat to medium. Cover and grill as above.) To serve, sprinkle fish and vegetables with snipped chervil.

Nutrition Facts per serving: 352 cal., 6 g total fat (1 g sat. fat), 42 mg chol., 266 mg sodium, 48 g carbo., 5 g fiber, 28 g pro.

mahi mahi WITH VEGETABLE SLAW

Prep: 15 minutes
Grill: 4 to 6 minutes
Makes: 4 servings

- 4 5- to 6-ounce fresh or frozen mahi mahi or pike fillets, ½ to ¾ inch thick
- 1 teaspoon finely shredded lime peel (set aside)
- ¼ cup lime juice
- ¼ cup snipped fresh cilantro
- 3 tablespoons olive oil
- 1 tablespoon honey
- 1 fresh jalapeño pepper, seeded and finely chopped
- 3 cloves garlic, minced
- ⅛ teaspoon salt
- 1½ cups packaged shredded cabbage with carrot (coleslaw mix)
- 1 cup shredded jicama

1 Thaw fish, if frozen. Rinse fish; pat dry. Place fish in a shallow dish. For dressing, in a small bowl combine lime juice, cilantro, oil, honey, jalapeño pepper, garlic, and salt; divide in half. Stir lime peel into 1 portion of dressing. Pour dressing with lime peel over fish; turn fish to coat. Cover; marinate at room temperature for 30 minutes.

2 For slaw, in a medium bowl combine cabbage mixture and jicama. Pour remaining dressing over slaw; toss to coat. Cover and chill until ready to serve.

3 Drain fish, discarding marinade. Place fish in a greased grill basket, tucking under any thin edges. For a charcoal grill, grill fish on the rack of an uncovered grill directly over medium coals until fish flakes easily when tested with a fork (allow 4 to 6 minutes per ½-inch thickness of fish), turning basket once halfway through grilling. (For a gas grill, preheat grill. Reduce heat to medium. Place fish on grill rack over heat. Cover and grill as above.) Serve fish with slaw.

Nutrition Facts per serving: 276 cal., 10 g total fat (1 g sat. fat), 67 mg chol., 130 mg sodium, 12 g carbo., 1 g fiber, 34 g pro.

halibut WITH CHUTNEY CREAM SAUCE

This velvety rich sauce makes a perfect partner to any type of white fish.

Prep: 20 minutes
Grill: 4 minutes per ½-inch thickness
Makes: 4 servings

- 4 fresh or frozen halibut steaks (about 1¾ pounds)
- 1 tablespoon lime juice
- Salt
- Black pepper
- 1 tablespoon finely chopped shallot
- ½ cup mango chutney
- ⅓ cup dry white wine
- 2 tablespoons whipping cream
- ½ cup butter, cut into 8 slices
- 1 mango, seeded, peeled, and sliced
- Sliced green onions

1 Thaw halibut, if frozen. Rinse fish; pat dry with paper towels. Brush with lime juice and sprinkle with salt and black pepper.

2 Lightly grease or coat with nonstick spray an unheated grill rack. For a charcoal grill, grill fish on the greased rack of an uncovered grill directly over medium coals for 4 to 6 minutes per ½-inch thickness or until fish flakes easily when tested with a fork, turning once. (For a gas grill, preheat grill. Reduce heat to medium. Place fish on greased grill rack over heat. Cover and grill as above.)

3 Meanwhile, for sauce, in a small saucepan stir together shallot, chutney, and wine. Bring to boiling; reduce heat. Boil gently, uncovered, for 5 minutes or until thickened, stirring occasionally. Add cream; heat through. Whisk in butter, one piece at a time, until melted. Serve fish with sauce and mango slices; sprinkle with green onions.

Nutrition Facts per serving: 562 cal., 32 g total fat (18 g sat. fat), 139 mg chol., 517 mg sodium, 24 g carbo., 2 g fiber, 43 g pro.

tuna and bean SALAD

Prep: 30 minutes
Cook: 2 minutes
Grill: 8 minutes
Stand: 1 hour
Makes: 6 servings

- 1 pound dried cannellini beans (white kidney beans) or three 19-ounce cans cannellini beans, rinsed and drained
- ½ cup fresh marjoram sprigs
- 6 tablespoons extra virgin olive oil
- Kosher salt and freshly ground black pepper
- 2 to 4 anchovy fillets, drained
- ⅓ cup finely chopped parsley
- 3 tablespoons drained capers
- 2 cloves garlic, minced
- 1 teaspoon Dijon-style mustard
- 6 tablespoons lemon juice (2 lemons)
- ¼ cup extra virgin olive oil
- 6 4-ounce fresh tuna steaks, about ¾ inch thick
- 6 ½ inch slices red onions (2 large)
- Fresh marjoram sprigs (optional)

1 Rinse dried beans, if using. In a Dutch oven combine beans and 8 cups water. Bring to boiling; reduce heat. Simmer, covered, for 2 minutes. Remove from heat. Let stand, covered, for 1 hour. (Or place beans in water in Dutch oven. Cover and let soak in a cool place for 6 to 8 hours or overnight.) Drain and rinse beans. Return beans to Dutch oven. Stir in 8 cups fresh water; add ½ cup marjoram sprigs and 1 tablespoon of olive oil. Bring to boiling; reduce heat. Simmer, covered, about 2 hours or until tender. Drain, discarding marjoram sprigs. Cool slightly.

2 Toss cooked beans with 4 tablespoons olive oil; season with salt and pepper. Cover; set aside. (If using canned beans, in a saucepan stir together beans, 1½ to 2 tablespoons snipped fresh marjoram, 4 tablespoons olive oil, and salt and pepper to taste. Cook over medium heat until heated through, stirring occasionally; cover and keep warm.)

3 For vinaigrette, in a small bowl mash anchovy fillets with a fork. Add parsley, capers, garlic, and mustard; mix thoroughly. Stir in 2 tablespoons of the lemon juice. Add the ¼ cup olive oil, whisking to combine ingredients. Season to taste with additional salt. Set aside.

4 Brush the tuna and onion slices with remaining 1 tablespoon olive oil; sprinkle lightly with additional salt and pepper. For a charcoal grill, place fish and onions on the grill rack directly over medium coals. Grill, uncovered, for 8 to 9 minutes or until tuna is slightly pink in center and onion is tender, turning once halfway through grilling. (For a gas grill, preheat grill. Reduce heat to medium. Place tuna and onions on the grill rack over heat. Cover and grill as above.)

5 To serve, spoon beans onto six serving plates. Drizzle beans with remaining 4 tablespoons lemon juice. Place a fish fillet on each plate. Drizzle each serving with vinaigrette. Serve with red onion slices. Sprinkle with additional marjoram sprigs, if desired.

Nutrition Facts per serving: 603 cal., 25 g total fat (4 g sat. fat), 52 mg chol., 734 mg sodium, 53 g carbo., 16 g fiber, 44 g pro.

sea bass WITH WILTED GREENS

A refreshing citrus vinaigrette dresses the fish as well as the wilted spinach greens.

Prep: 25 minutes
Marinate: 30 minutes
Grill: 4 minutes per ½-inch thickness
Makes: 4 servings

- 4 4- to 5-ounces fresh or frozen sea bass, tilapia, or catfish fillets
- 1 teaspoon finely shredded orange peel
- ⅓ cup orange juice
- 3 tablespoons olive oil
- 1 tablespoon snipped fresh chives
- 2 cloves garlic, minced
- ¼ teaspoon salt
- 6 cups torn fresh spinach
- ⅔ cup red grape tomatoes or red teardrop tomatoes, halved

1 Thaw fish, if frozen. Rinse fish; pat dry with paper towels. For vinaigrette, in a screw-top jar combine orange peel, orange juice, oil, chives, garlic, and salt. Cover and shake well.

2 Place fish in a shallow dish. Pour half of the vinaigrette over fish; turn fish to coat. Cover and marinate in the refrigerator for 30 minutes. Drain fish; discard marinade.

3 Place fish in a well-greased grill basket, tucking under any thin edges. For a charcoal grill, grill fish on the rack of an uncovered grill directly over medium coals for 4 to 6 minutes per ½-inch thickness of fish or until fish flakes easily when tested with a fork, turning basket once. Remove fish from basket; keep warm. (For a gas grill, preheat grill. Reduce heat to medium. Place fish on greased grill basket. Place basket on grill rack over heat. Cover and grill as above.)

4 In a large skillet heat remaining vinaigrette over medium heat. Add spinach, gently tossing to coat. Remove from heat. Stir in tomatoes. To serve, divide spinach mixture evenly among four dinner plates. Top with fish.

Nutrition Facts per serving: 201 cal., 10 g total fat (2 g sat. fat), 46 mg chol., 231 mg sodium, 5 g carbo., 1 g fiber, 23 g pro.

stacked ASIAN-STYLE GROUPER

Egg roll wrappers are fried and layered with fish, avocados, and tomatoes. The finished dish is drizzled with wasabi-spiked mayonnaise.

Prep: 30 minutes
Marinate: 30 minutes to 1 hour
Grill: 4 minutes per ½-inch thickness
Makes: 4 servings

- 4   4- to 6-ounce fresh or frozen grouper, red snapper, or orange roughy fillets, ½ to 1 inch thick
- ¼   cup mayonnaise
- ½   teaspoon wasabi paste
- 2   tablespoons rice vinegar
- 2   tablespoons soy sauce
- 1   tablespoon minced garlic
- ¼   teaspoon ground ginger
- 4   egg roll wrappers
-     Cooking oil
- 2   medium tomatoes, sliced
- 2   teaspoons toasted sesame oil
- 1   medium avocado, peeled, seeded, and cut into ¼-inch slices
- 1   teaspoon toasted sesame seeds (optional)
-     Sliced green onions (optional)

1 Thaw fish, if frozen. Rinse fish; pat dry with paper towels. Combine mayonnaise and wasabi paste in a resealable plastic bag. Seal bag and chill until ready to use.

2 For marinade, in a small bowl combine vinegar, soy sauce, garlic, and ginger. Place fish in a resealable plastic bag set in a shallow dish. Pour marinade over fish in bag. Seal bag. Marinate in refrigerator 30 minutes to 1 hour, turning bag occasionally.

3 Meanwhile, in a large skillet fry egg roll wrappers, one at a time, in ½ inch of hot oil for 30 to 45 seconds or until golden, turning once. Remove from oil. Drain on paper towels. Remove fish from marinade; discard marinade. Place fish fillets in a well-greased grill basket, tucking under any thin edges.

4 For a charcoal grill, grill fish on the rack of an uncovered grill directly over medium coals for 4 to 6 minutes per ½-inch thickness or until fish flakes easily when tested with a fork, turning basket once halfway through grilling. (For a gas grill, preheat grill. Reduce heat to medium. Place fish on grill rack over heat. Cover and grill as above.)

5 To assemble, for each serving, place a fried egg roll wrapper on a plate. Cut a small hole in the corner of the plastic bag containing mayonnaise mixture; drizzle some over top of egg roll wrapper. Top with a fish fillet and tomato slices. Drizzle with ½ teaspoon of the sesame oil. Top with ¼ of the avocado slices. If desired, sprinkle with ¼ teaspoon toasted sesame seeds and green onions. Repeat for each serving.

Nutrition Facts per serving: 448 cal., 26 g total fat (4 g sat. fat), 50 mg chol., 787 mg sodium, 25 g carbo., 3 g fiber, 28 g pro.

caramelized salmon WITH CITRUS SALSA

Fragrant and delicious, this make-ahead recipe is especially impressive because the orange-scented sugar rub turns a rich golden brown during grilling.

Prep: 20 minutes
Marinate: 8 to 24 hours
Grill: 15 minutes
Makes: 4 servings

- 1   1½-pound fresh or frozen salmon or halibut fillet (with skin), 1 inch thick
- 2   tablespoons sugar
- 1½ teaspoons finely shredded orange peel
- 1   teaspoon salt
- ¼   teaspoon freshly ground black pepper
- 1   teaspoon finely shredded orange peel
- 2   oranges, peeled, sectioned, and coarsely chopped
- 1   cup chopped fresh pineapple or canned crushed pineapple, drained
- 2   tablespoons snipped fresh cilantro
- 1   tablespoon finely chopped shallots
- 1   fresh jalapeño pepper, seeded and finely chopped

1 Thaw fish, if frozen. Rinse fish; pat dry with paper towels. Place fish, skin side down, in a shallow dish. For rub, in a small bowl stir together sugar, the 1½ teaspoons orange peel, the salt, and black pepper. Sprinkle rub evenly over fish (not on skin side); rub in with your fingers. Cover and marinate in the refrigerator for 8 to 24 hours.

2 Meanwhile, for salsa, in a small bowl stir together the 1 teaspoon orange peel, the oranges, pineapple, cilantro, shallot, and jalapeño pepper. Cover and chill until ready to serve or for up to 24 hours. Drain fish, discarding liquid.

3 For a charcoal grill, arrange medium-hot coals around a drip pan. Test for medium heat above the pan. Place fish, skin side down, on greased grill rack over drip pan. Cover and grill about 12 minutes or until fish flakes easily when tested with a fork. (For a gas grill, preheat grill. Reduce heat to medium. Adjust for indirect cooking. Grill as above.)

4 To serve, cut fish into 4 serving-size pieces, cutting to but not through the skin. Carefully slip a metal spatula between fish and skin, lifting fish up and away from skin. Serve fish with salsa.

Nutrition Facts per serving: 145 cal., 4 g total fat (1 g sat. fat), 20 mg chol., 424 mg sodium, 10 g carbo., 1 g fiber, 17 g pro.

salmon and asparagus
WITH GARDEN MAYONNAISE

A spoonful of lemony herbed mayonnaise puts the finishing touch on a bistro-style plate presentation.

Prep: 10 minutes
Grill: 8 minutes
Makes: 4 servings

- 4   6- to 8-ounce skinless salmon fillets, cut 1 inch thick
- 1   pound asparagus spears
- 1   tablespoon olive oil
-     Sea salt or salt
-     Freshly ground black pepper
- ½   cup finely chopped celery (1 stalk)
- ¼   cup thinly sliced green onions (2)
- ⅓   cup mayonnaise
- 1   tablespoon lemon juice
- 2   teaspoons snipped fresh tarragon or ½ teaspoon dried tarragon, crushed
-     Lemon wedges (optional)

1 Rinse fish; pat dry with paper towels. Snap off and discard woody bases from asparagus spears. Brush asparagus and both sides of each salmon fillet lightly with some of the oil. Season asparagus and salmon with salt and pepper.

2 Grease the unheated grill rack. For a charcoal grill, place salmon on the greased grill rack directly over medium coals. Place asparagus on grill rack next to salmon. Grill, uncovered, for 8 to 12 minutes or until asparagus is tender and fish flakes easily when tested with a fork, turning fish once halfway through grilling, and turning asparagus occasionally. (For a gas grill, preheat grill. Reduce heat to medium. Place fish and asparagus on grill rack over heat. Cover and grill as above.)

3 Meanwhile, in a small bowl stir together celery, green onions, mayonnaise, lemon juice, and tarragon.

4 To serve, arrange asparagus on four serving plates. Top each serving with a salmon fillet. Spoon mayonnaise mixture on top of salmon. Serve with lemon wedges, if desired.

Nutrition Facts per serving: 501 cal., 37 g total fat (7 g sat. fat), 107 mg chol., 313 mg sodium, 6 g carbo., 3 g fiber, 37 g pro.

glazed PROSCIUTTO-WRAPPED SHRIMP

Prosciutto, an Italian ham, is a perfect wrap for quick-cooked shrimp because it toughens with long cooking times. The bourbon barbecue sauce is a bold complement.

Prep: 30 minutes
Grill: 6 to 9 minutes
Makes: 4 servings

- ½ cup Bourbon grilling sauce
- ½ teaspoon chili powder
- 24 fresh or frozen large shrimp in shells
- 8 slices prosciutto
- Lemon or Parmesan Couscous* (optional)

1 Thaw shrimp, if frozen. Peel and devein shrimp. Rinse shrimp; pat dry with paper towels. Set aside. In a small bowl stir together grilling sauce and chili powder. Cut each prosciutto slice lengthwise into three strips. Wrap 1 strip prosciutto around each shrimp. Thread shrimp on four long metal skewers, leaving a ¼-inch space between each piece. Brush shrimp with sauce.

2 For a charcoal grill, grill shrimp on the rack of an uncovered grill directly over medium coals for 6 to 9 minutes or until shrimp are opaque, turning once halfway through grilling and brushing occasionally with sauce. (For a gas grill, preheat grill. Reduce heat to medium. Place shrimp on grill rack over heat. Cover and grill as above.)

3 If desired, serve shrimp over Lemon or Parmesan Couscous.

***Lemon or Parmesan Couscous:** Prepare a 10-ounce package of couscous according to package directions. Stir in 2 teaspoons finely shredded lemon peel or ½ cup finely shredded Parmesan cheese.

Nutrition Facts per serving: 195 cal., 4 g total fat (1 g sat. fat), 207 mg chol., 932 mg sodium, 5 g carbo., 0 g fiber, 32 g pro.

grilled shrimp IN COCONUT MILK SAUCE

Prep: 25 minutes
Chill: 30 minutes
Cook: 15 minutes
Grill: 5 minutes
Makes: 4 servings

- 1 pound fresh or frozen extra-large shrimp
- 2 teaspoons lime juice
- 1 malagueta, tabasco, or bird chile pepper or chile de arbol, finely chopped*
- 2 cloves garlic, minced
- Salt
- Freshly ground black pepper
- ½ cup chopped red sweet pepper
- ¼ cup finely chopped onion
- 1 tablespoon olive oil
- 1 cup chopped tomato (2 medium)
- ½ cup unsweetened coconut milk
- 1 tablespoon tomato paste
- Salt
- Snipped fresh parsley or cilantro

1 Thaw shrimp, if frozen. Peel and devein shrimp. Rinse shrimp; pat dry with paper towels. In a medium bowl combine shrimp, lime juice, and half of the finely chopped chile pepper, half of the garlic; add salt and black pepper to taste. Toss to coat. Cover and marinate in the refrigerator for 30 minutes to 1 hour, stirring occasionally.

2 For sauce, in a medium skillet, cook sweet pepper, onion, remaining chile pepper, and remaining garlic in hot oil over medium heat about 10 minutes or until tender, stirring occasionally. Add tomato, coconut milk, and tomato paste. Bring to boiling; reduce heat. Simmer, uncovered, about 5 minutes or until sauce reaches desired consistency. Season to taste with salt. Set aside and keep warm.

3 Thread shrimp onto four long metal skewers. Transfer skewers to a baking sheet or tray. Grease an unheated grill rack. For a charcoal grill, place skewers on the greased rack directly over medium coals. Grill, uncovered, for 7 to 9 minutes or until shrimp are opaque, turning once halfway through grilling. (For a gas grill, preheat grill. Reduce heat to medium. Place skewers on greased grill rack over heat. Cover and grill as above.)

4 Spoon the sauce onto a platter or divide it among four shallow bowls and place shrimp skewers on top. Sprinkle with snipped parsley.

Nutrition Facts per serving: 195 cal., 10 g total fat (6 g sat. fat), 129 mg chol., 327 mg sodium, 6 g carbo., 1 g fiber, 19 g pro.

***Note:** Because hot chile peppers contain volatile oils that can burn your skin and eyes, avoid direct contact with chiles as much as possible. When working with chile peppers, wear plastic or rubber gloves. If your bare hands do touch the chile peppers, wash your hands well with soap and water.

thai-style SEAFOOD KABOBS

While the coconut milk-and-lime marinade is doing its magic, you have time to make a simple peanut sauce. Just minutes on the grill and the kabobs are ready to enjoy.

Prep: 20 minutes
Marinate: 30 minutes
Grill: 5 minutes
Stand: 30 minutes
Makes: 4 to 6 servings

- 8 ounces fresh or frozen peeled and deveined medium shrimp
- 8 ounces fresh or frozen sea scallops
- ¼ cup purchased unsweetened coconut milk
- 2 tablespoons lime juice
- 1 tablespoon soy sauce
- ⅓ cup purchased unsweetened coconut milk
- ¼ cup peanut butter
- 2 tablespoons snipped fresh cilantro
- 1 tablespoon thinly sliced green onion
- 1 tablespoon lime juice
- ½ teaspoon chile paste or ⅛ teaspoon crushed red pepper

1 Thaw shrimp and scallops, if frozen. Rinse and pat dry with paper towels. Place in a medium bowl.

2 For marinade, in a small bowl combine the ¼ cup coconut milk, the 2 tablespoons lime juice, and the soy sauce. Pour marinade over shrimp and scallops, stirring to coat. Cover and marinate at room temperature for 30 minutes, stirring once.

3 Meanwhile, for sauce, in a small bowl whisk together the ⅓ cup coconut milk, the peanut butter, cilantro, green onion, the 1 tablespoon lime juice, and the chile paste. Cover and let stand at room temperature for 30 minutes.

4 Drain shrimp and scallops, discarding marinade. On long metal skewers alternately thread shrimp and scallops, leaving a ¼-inch space between pieces.

5 Lightly grease or coat with nonstick cooking spray an unheated grill rack. For a charcoal grill, grill kabobs on the greased rack of an uncovered grill directly over medium coals for 5 to 8 minutes or until shrimp and scallops are opaque, turning once halfway through grilling. (For a gas grill, preheat grill. Reduce heat to medium. Place skewers on greased grill rack over heat. Cover and grill as above.) Serve seafood with sauce.

Nutrition Facts per serving: 247 cal., 15 g total fat (6 g sat. fat), 84 mg chol., 350 mg sodium, 7 g carbo., 1 g fiber, 23 g pro.

soy-lime SCALLOPS WITH LEEKS

The sugar in the lime halves caramelizes for a sharp-sweet finishing touch.

Prep: 10 minutes
Marinate: 30 minutes
Grill: 8 minutes
Makes: 4 servings

- 1 pound fresh or frozen sea scallops
- ¼ cup soy sauce
- ¼ cup rice vinegar
- 8 baby leeks
- 12 medium green or red scallions, or green onions
- 1 medium lime, halved
- Black sesame seeds (optional)
- ¼ cup butter, melted

1 Thaw scallops, if frozen. Rinse scallops; pat dry with paper towels. For marinade, in a small bowl combine soy sauce and rice vinegar; set aside.

2 Trim root end and green tops of leeks. Rinse leeks thoroughly to remove any grit. Cut the small leek (if using) lengthwise into quarters; insert a wooden pick crosswise through each leek quarter to hold layers together when grilling. Or trim the baby leeks.

3 Place leeks, scallops, and scallions in a resealable plastic bag set in a shallow dish. Add marinade. Seal bag; turn to coat scallops and vegetables. Marinate in refrigerator for 30 minutes.

4 Remove scallops, leeks, and scallions from bag. Discard marinade. For a charcoal grill, place leeks, scallops, scallions, and lime halves (cut sides down) on the rack of an uncovered grill directly over medium coals. Grill for 8 to 10 minutes or until scallops are opaque, turning scallops and vegetables occasionally. Remove any scallions from grill rack before they over brown. (For a gas grill, preheat grill. Reduce heat to medium. Place leeks, scallions, and scallops on grill rack over heat. Grill as above.)

5 To serve, transfer leeks and scallions to serving plates. Top with scallops. Using grilling tongs, remove limes from grill and squeeze over scallops. If desired, sprinkle with black sesame seeds. Serve with melted butter.

Nutrition Facts per serving: 255 cal., 13 g total fat (6 g sat. fat), 70 mg chol., 515 mg sodium, 13 g carbo., 2 g fiber, 21 g pro.

zucchini CRAB CAKES

Carefully pick through the crabmeat and remove any small bits of shell. Buy crabmeat in cans—it's less expensive than fresh lump crabmeat.

Prep: 20 minutes
Grill: 8 minutes
Makes: 8 crab cakes
(4 servings)

- 1 cup coarsely shredded zucchini
- ¼ cup thinly sliced green onions (2)
- 2 teaspoons cooking oil
- 1 egg, beaten
- ⅔ cup seasoned fine dry bread crumbs
- 1 tablespoon Dijon-style mustard
- 1 teaspoon snipped fresh thyme or ½ teaspoon dried thyme, crushed
- ⅛ to ¼ teaspoon cayenne pepper
- 8 ounces fresh lump crabmeat (1½ cups) or two 6-ounce cans crabmeat, drained, flaked, and cartilage removed
- 2 large red and/or yellow tomatoes, sliced ¼ inch thick
- Tomato Sour Cream Sauce*
- Lemon and/or lime wedges (optional)

1 In a medium skillet cook zucchini and green onions in hot oil over medium-high heat for 3 to 5 minutes or until vegetables are just tender and liquid is evaporated. Cool slightly.

2 In a large bowl combine egg, bread crumbs, mustard, thyme, and cayenne pepper. Add crabmeat and the zucchini mixture; mix well. Using about ¼ cup mixture per crab cake, shape into eight ½-inch-thick patties.

3 Lightly grease an unheated grill rack or coat with nonstick cooking spray. For a charcoal grill, grill crab cakes on the greased rack of an uncovered grill directly over medium coals for 8 to 10 minutes or until golden, turning once. For a gas grill, preheat grill. Reduce heat to medium. Place crab cakes on greased grill rack over heat. Cover; grill as above.

4 To serve, arrange tomato slices and crab cakes on plates. Serve with Tomato-Sour Cream Sauce and, if desired, lemon wedges.

***Tomato-Sour Cream Sauce:** In a small bowl stir together ½ cup dairy sour cream, ¼ cup finely chopped yellow or red tomato, 1 tablespoon lemon or lime juice, and ⅛ teaspoon seasoned salt. Cover and chill until serving time. Makes ¾ cup.

Nutrition Facts per serving: 243 cal., 10 g total fat (4 g sat. fat), 120 mg chol., 835 mg sodium, 20 g carbo., 1 g fiber, 18 g pro.

rock lobster TAILS

Prep: 15 minutes
Grill: 11 minutes
Makes: 4 servings

- 4 6-ounces fresh or frozen rock lobster tails
- 2 tablespoons olive oil
- ½ teaspoon finely shredded lemon or lime peel
- 4 teaspoons lemon or lime juice
- 2 cloves garlic, minced
- 1 teaspoon chili powder
- ½ cup mayonnaise or salad dressing
- 1 teaspoon snipped fresh dill or ¼ teaspoon dried dill
-    Lemon or lime wedges (optional)

1 Thaw rock lobster tails, if frozen. Rinse lobster; pat dry with paper towels. Using kitchen shears or a large sharp knife, cut each lobster tail in half through center of hard top shell, meat of lobster tail, and undershells. Set lobster tails aside.

2 In a small bowl combine oil, 2 teaspoons of the lemon juice, the garlic, and chili powder; brush on exposed lobster meat, reserving some of the lemon juice mixture.

3 For a charcoal grill, grill lobster tails cut sides down on the rack of an uncovered grill directly over medium heat for 6 minutes. Turn lobster tails; brush with reserved lemon juice mixture. Grill 5 to 8 minutes more or until meat is opaque in the center. Do not overcook. (For a gas grill, preheat grill. Reduce heat to medium. Place lobster tails on grill rack over heat. Cover and grill as above.)

4 Meanwhile, for sauce, combine mayonnaise, dill, lemon peel, and remaining 2 teaspoons lemon juice. Serve lobster with sauce and, if desired, lemon wedges.

Nutrition Facts per serving: 367 cal., 30 g total fat (4 g sat. fat), 128 mg chol., 462 mg sodium, 2 g carbo., 0 g fiber, 22 g pro.

clam BAKE

Although traditional clam bakes are cooked in a pit on the beach, you can enjoy this version in your backyard.

Prep: 20 minutes
Soak: 45 minutes total
Cook: 20 minutes
Makes: 4 servings

- 1 pound littleneck clams
- 1 pound mussels
- 1 pound cooked smoked chorizo sausage, sliced ½-inch thick (optional)
- 1 pound small round red potatoes, cut into 1-inch pieces
- 4 ears fresh corn, husks and silks removed
- 4 6- to 8-ounce lobster tails
- ½ cup butter, melted

1 Scrub clams and mussels in shells under cold running water. Remove beards from mussels, if present. Place clams and mussels in a large bowl; add ⅓ cup salt and enough cold water to cover. Soak for 15 minutes; drain. Repeat two more times. Rinse in fresh cold water.

2 Place clams and mussels in the bottom of a 13x9x3-inch disposable foil pan. Place chorizo (if desired), potatoes, and corn on top of shellfish. Place lobster tails on top. Cover pan with foil, sealing well.

3 For a charcoal grill, grill foil pan on the rack of an uncovered grill directly over medium coals for 20 to 30 minutes or until potatoes are tender. (For a gas grill, preheat grill. Reduce heat to medium. Place foil pan on the grill rack over heat. Cover and grill as above.)

4 Transfer clam mixture to a serving platter, reserving cooking liquid. Discard clams and mussels that don't open. Serve seafood and vegetables with butter and cooking liquid.

Nutrition Facts per serving: 564 cal., 34 g total fat (17 g sat. fat), 166 mg chol., 647 mg sodium, 44 g carbo., 4 g fiber, 25 g pro.

linguine and clams IN
HERBED WINE SAUCE

Prep: 30 minutes
Grill: 10 minutes
Stand: 45 minutes
Makes: 4 servings

- 2 dozen live clams
- 1 cup salt
- 3 tablespoons olive oil
- 6 cloves garlic, minced
- 2 medium onions, sliced
- 4 anchovy fillets, finely chopped, or ¼ teaspoon anchovy paste
- ½ cup dry white wine
- ¼ teaspoon sea salt
- ¼ teaspoon coarsely ground black pepper
- ⅛ to ¼ teaspoon crushed red pepper
- 6 medium plum tomatoes, seeded and finely chopped
- ¼ cup fresh snipped basil
- 1 tablespoon fresh snipped oregano
- 2 tablespoons olive oil
- 8 ounces dried linguine or spaghetti
- 8 sprigs fresh thyme
- 2 bay leaves
- 4 slices French bread

1 Scrub clams in shells under cold running water. In an 8-quart Dutch oven combine 4 quarts cold water and ⅓ cup of the salt; add clams. Let stand for 15 minutes; drain and rinse. Using fresh water and salt, repeat two more times.

2 For sauce, heat 3 tablespoons of the olive oil in a large skillet over medium heat. Cook garlic in the hot oil about 30 seconds. Add onions and anchovies; cook, stirring occasionally, for 4 to 5 minutes or until onions are tender. Add wine, sea salt, black pepper, and crushed red pepper; continue cooking 2 minutes more. Remove from heat. Stir in tomatoes, 2 tablespoons of the basil, and the oregano. Set aside.

3 Meanwhile, prepare linguine according to package directions. Toss hot pasta with remaining 2 tablespoons olive oil; cover and keep warm.

4 Place the clams in a 2-quart disposable foil pan. Tie thyme sprigs and bay leaves together in a bundle with 100-percent-cotton string. Add thyme and bay leaves to pan. Add sauce. Cover pan with foil; seal tightly.

5 For a charcoal grill, grill clams in foil pan on a grill rack directly over medium-hot coals for 10 to 12 minutes or until shells open and sauce is hot. (For a gas grill, preheat grill. Reduce heat to medium-high. Place pan on a grill rack. Cover and grill as above.) Discard any clams that do not open. Discard thyme sprigs and bay leaves. Sprinkle with remaining 2 tablespoons basil. Serve immediately with the linguine and slices of French bread.

Nutrition Facts per serving: 551 cal., 20 g total fat (3 g sat. fat), 23 mg chol., 448 mg sodium, 69 g carbo., 5 g fiber, 20 g pro.

simply
SMOKIN'

Prosciutto-Stuffed Pork, *recipe page 193*

texans' BEEF BRISKET

Prep: 30 minutes
Soak: 1 hour
Smoke: 5 hours
Makes: 12 servings

- 6 to 8 mesquite, hickory, or pecan wood chunks
- Vinegar Mop Sauce*
- 1 3- to 3½-pound fresh beef brisket
- 2 teaspoons seasoned salt
- 1 teaspoon paprika
- 1 teaspoon chili powder
- 1 teaspoon garlic pepper
- ½ teaspoon ground cumin
- Spicy Beer Sauce**
- 12 kaiser rolls, split and toasted (optional)

1 At least 1 hour before smoke cooking, soak wood chunks in enough water to cover. Drain before using.

2 Prepare Vinegar Mop Sauce; set aside. Trim fat from meat. For rub, in a small bowl combine seasoned salt, paprika, chili powder, garlic pepper, and cumin. Sprinkle mixture evenly over meat; rub in with your fingers.

3 In a smoker arrange preheated coals, drained wood chunks, and water pan according to the manufacturer's directions. Pour water into pan. Place meat on grill rack over water pan. Cover; smoke for 5 to 6 hours or until meat is tender, brushing occasionally with Vinegar Mop Sauce during the last hour of smoking. Add additional coals and water as needed to maintain temperature and moisture.

4 To serve, thinly slice meat across the grain. Serve meat with Spicy Beer Sauce. If desired, serve meat and sauce in Kaiser rolls.

***Vinegar Mop Sauce:** In a small bowl stir together ¼ cup beer, 4 teaspoons Worcestershire sauce, 1 tablespoon cooking oil, 1 tablespoon vinegar, ½ teaspoon jalapeño mustard or other hot-style mustard, and a few dashes bottled hot pepper sauce.

****Spicy Beer Sauce:** In a medium saucepan melt 2 tablespoons butter or margarine. Add ¾ cup chopped, seeded, peeled tomato (1 large); ½ cup chopped onion (1 medium); and ½ cup chopped green sweet pepper. Cook about 5 minutes or until onion is tender, stirring occasionally. Stir in 1 cup bottled chili sauce, ½ cup beer, ½ cup cider vinegar, 2 tablespoons brown sugar, 1 to 2 tablespoons chopped chipotle peppers in adobo sauce, 1¼ teaspoons black pepper, and ½ teaspoon salt. Bring to boiling; reduce heat. Boil gently, uncovered, about 10 minutes or until reduced to about 2¼ cups.

Nutrition Facts per serving: 253 cal., 12 g total fat (4 g sat. fat), 77 mg chol., 770 mg sodium, 11 g carbo., 2 g fiber, 24 g pro.

smoked brisket WITH BLACK BEAN AND CORN SALSA

Leftovers of this smoky meat and freshly made salsa make a terrific taco filling. Add shreds of lettuce and a sprinkling of cheese to complete your tasty tacos.

Prep: 40 minutes
Marinate: 6 hours
Soak: 1 hour
Smoke: 5 hours
Makes: 8 to 10 servings

1	3- to 3½-pound beef brisket
1	12-ounce bottle or can beer
¾	cup lime juice
½	cup chopped onion
3	tablespoons cooking oil
3	tablespoons steak sauce
2	teaspoons chili powder
2	teaspoons ground cumin
2	teaspoons bottled minced garlic
6	to 8 oak or hickory wood chunks
	Black Bean and Corn Salsa*

1 Trim fat from brisket. Place brisket in a large resealable plastic bag. For marinade, in a medium bowl combine the beer, lime juice, onion, oil, steak sauce, chili powder, cumin, and garlic; pour over brisket. Seal bag. Refrigerate for 6 to 24 hours, turning bag occasionally.

2 For at least 1 hour before smoke cooking, soak the wood chunks in enough water to cover. Drain before using. Drain brisket, discarding the marinade.

3 In a smoker arrange preheated coals, drained wood chunks, and water pan according to the manufacturers directions. Pour water into pan. Place brisket on the grill rack over the water pan. Cover and smoke for 5 to 6 hours or until tender. Add additional coals and water as needed to maintain temperature and moisture.

4 To serve, thinly slice brisket across the grain. Serve brisket with Black Bean and Corn Salsa.

*Black Bean and Corn Salsa: In a large bowl, combine 3 cups chopped, seeded tomatoes; one 15-ounce can black beans, rinsed and drained; 1 cup frozen whole kernel corn, thawed; ¼ cup thinly sliced green onions (2); 3 tablespoons snipped fresh cilantro; 2 tablespoons cooking oil; 2 tablespoons lime juice; ½ teaspoon salt; ¼ teaspoon ground cumin; ¼ teaspoon ground black pepper; and 1 fresh jalapeño chile pepper, seeded and finely chopped. Cover and chill for 6 to 24 hours.

Nutrition Facts per serving: 381 cal., 17 g total fat (5 g sat. fat), 83 mg chol., 429 mg sodium, 17 g carbo., 4 g fiber, 40 g pro.

spiced AND SASSY BEEF RIBS

Beef ribs have hearty flavor that provides many options for rubbing and smoking. Apply the exotic rub and then chill the meat for anywhere from eight hours to two days.

Prep: 30 minutes
Chill: 8 to 48 hours
Smoke: 2½ hours
Soak: 1 hour
Makes: 4 servings

- 4 pounds beef back ribs (about 8 ribs)
- 1 tablespoon paprika
- 1 tablespoon garlic salt
- 1 tablespoon finely cracked mixed peppercorns or 1½ teaspoons coarsely ground black pepper
- ½ teaspoon ground cumin
- ½ teaspoon dried thyme, crushed
- ½ teaspoon onion powder
- ¼ teaspoon ground coriander
- ⅛ teaspoon cayenne pepper
- ⅛ teaspoon ground cardamom
- 8 to 10 mesquite or hickory wood chunks
- 2 tablespoons cooking oil
- Mustard Dipping Sauce*

1 Trim fat from ribs. For rub, in a small bowl combine the paprika, garlic salt, peppercorns, cumin, thyme, onion powder, coriander, cayenne pepper, and cardamom. Sprinkle rub evenly over ribs; rub in with your fingers. Cover and chill for 8 to 48 hours.

2 For at least 1 hour before smoke cooking, soak wood chunks in enough water to cover. Drain before using.

3 In a smoker arrange preheated coals, drained wood chunks, and water pan according to the manufacturer's directions. Pour water into pan. Place ribs on the grill rack over the water pan. Smoke, covered, for 2½ to 3 hours or until tender. Add additional coals and water as needed to maintain temperature and moisture. Serve ribs with Mustard Dipping Sauce.

***Mustard Dipping Sauce:** In a small saucepan, whisk together ⅓ cup Dijon-style mustard, ¼ cup honey, ¼ cup apple juice, 4 teaspoons brown sugar, 1 tablespoon cider vinegar, and ⅛ teaspoon salt. Bring to boiling; reduce heat. Simmer, uncovered, for 3 minutes. Serve warm or chilled.

Nutrition Facts per serving: 393 cal., 25 g total fat (8 g sat. fat), 88 mg chol., 843 mg sodium, 2 g carbo., 1 g fiber, 38 g pro.

spicy HOISIN-HONEY RIBS

Thick and reddish brown in color, hoisin sauce is a sweet and spicy medley of soybeans, garlic, chile peppers, and spices.

Prep: 15 minutes
Soak: 1 hour
Marinate: 1 to 4 hours
Smoke: 3 hours
Makes: 4 servings

- 1 tablespoon paprika
- ½ teaspoon coarsely ground black pepper
- ¼ teaspoon onion salt
- 4 pounds pork loin back ribs
- 1 lime, halved
- 6 to 8 oak or hickory wood chunks
- 2 dried chipotle peppers or 1 to 2 tablespoons finely chopped canned chipotle peppers in adobo sauce
- ½ cup bottled hoisin sauce
- ¼ cup honey
- 2 tablespoons cider vinegar
- 2 tablespoons Dijon-style mustard
- 2 cloves garlic, minced

1 For rub, in a small bowl combine paprika, black pepper, and onion salt. Trim fat from ribs. Place ribs in a shallow dish. Squeeze and rub the cut surfaces of the lime halves over ribs. Sprinkle the rub evenly over ribs; rub in with your fingers. Cover and marinate in the refrigerator for 1 to 4 hours.

2 At least 1 hour before smoke cooking, soak wood chunks in enough water to cover. Drain before using.

3 In a smoker, arrange preheated coals, drained wood chunks, and water pan according to the manufacturer's directions. Pour water into pan. Place ribs, bone sides down, on the grill rack over water pan. (Or place ribs in a rib rack; place on grill rack.) Cover; smoke for 3 to 4 hours or until ribs are tender. Add additional coals and water as needed to maintain temperature and moisture.

4 Meanwhile, for sauce, if using dried chipotle peppers, soak them in warm water for 30 minutes; drain well and finely chop. In a small saucepan stir together the chipotle peppers in sauce or dried peppers, hoisin sauce, honey, vinegar, mustard, and garlic. Cook and stir over low heat until heated through.

5 Before serving, brush ribs with some of the sauce. Pass the remaining sauce.

Nutrition Facts per serving: 509 cal., 25 g total fat (8 g sat. fat), 110 mg chol., 898 mg sodium, 40 g carbo., 1 g fiber, 28 g pro.

applewood-smoked
PORK CHOPS

If you choose to use a purchased rub instead of the homemade version, select one that is not too high in sugar. Rubs high in sugar tend to overbrown during long cooking.

Prep: 30 minutes
Chill: 2 hour
Smoke: 1¾ hour
Soak: 1 hour
Makes: 4 servings

- 4 boneless pork top loin chops, cut 1½ inches thick
- 2 tablespoons purchased barbecue spice rub
- 6 to 8 apple, cherry, or orange wood chunks
- 1 tablespoon butter
- 1 medium apple, peeled, cored, and chopped
- ¼ cup chopped onion
- 1 small clove garlic, minced
- 3 tablespoons bourbon or apple juice
- 1 tablespoon apple cider vinegar
- ⅔ cup chicken stock or broth
- ⅓ cup yellow mustard
- 1 tablespoon Dijon-style mustard
- 2 tablespoons honey
- Salt and ground black pepper
- Apple cut into julienne strips (optional)

1 Trim fat from chops. Place chops in a single layer in a shallow dish. Sprinkle some of the spice rub evenly over both sides of each chop; rub in with your fingers. Cover and chill for 2 to 4 hours.

2 For at least 1 hour before smoke cooking, soak the wood chunks in enough water to cover. Drain before using.

3 In a smoker, arrange preheated coals, drained wood chunks, and water pan according to the manufacturer's directions. Pour water into pan. Place chops on the grill rack over water pan. Cover and smoke for 1¾ to 2¼ hours or until the juices run clear (160°F). Add additional coals and water as needed to maintain temperature and moisture.

4 Meanwhile, for mustard sauce, in a medium skillet, melt butter over medium heat. Add chopped apple, onion, and garlic. Cook over medium heat about 5 minutes or until onion is tender, stirring occasionally. Add bourbon and vinegar. Cook and stir over medium heat until liquid is reduced by half, about 1 minute. Add chicken stock; bring to boiling. Cook, uncovered, until liquid is reduced by half, about 3 to 4 minutes. Stir in mustards. Bring to boiling; reduce heat. Simmer, uncovered, for 1 minute, stirring often. Remove from heat; add honey. Season to taste with salt and black pepper. Carefully add sauce to a food processor or blender. Cover and process or blend until smooth. Serve warm sauce over chops. If desired, top with apple strips.

Nutrition Facts per serving: 594 cal., 21 g total fat (8 g sat. fat), 178 mg chol., 1,066 mg sodium, 20 g carbo., 2 g fiber, 71 g pro.

prosciutto-stuffed PORK

Prep: 10 minutes
Soak: 1 hour
Smoke: 1¾ hours
Stand: 10 minutes
Makes: 6 to 8 servings

- 6 to 8 hickory or oak wood chunks
- 1 2- to 2½-pound boneless pork top loin roast (single loin)
- 2 tablespoons olive oil
- 1 to 2 tablespoons snipped fresh rosemary or 1 to 2 teaspoons dried rosemary, crushed
- 3 ounces thinly sliced prosciutto or dried beef
- 3 cups spinach leaves, stems removed
- 2 teaspoons crushed peppercorns (optional)
- Peach wedges, fresh Italian parsley sprigs, and fresh rosemary sprigs (optional)

1 At least 1 hour before smoke cooking, soak wood chunks in enough water to cover. Drain before using.

2 Trim fat from meat. To butterfly the meat, make a lengthwise cut down the center of the meat, cutting to within ½ inch of the other side, but not through it. Starting at the center of the meat, make one horizontal slit to the right, cutting within ½ inch of the other side. Repeat on the left side of center.

3 Brush the surface of meat with oil; sprinkle with rosemary. Cover with prosciutto and spinach. Starting from a short side, roll up into a spiral. Tie with 100-percent-cotton kitchen string. If desired, brush meat with additional oil and sprinkle with peppercorns. Insert a meat thermometer into center of meat.

4 In a smoker arrange preheated coals, drained wood chunks, and water pan according to the manufacturer's directions. Pour water into pan. Place meat on the grill rack over water pan. Cover; smoke for 1¾ to 2 hours or until meat thermometer registers 155°F. Add additional coals and water as needed to maintain temperature and moisture. Remove meat from smoker. Cover meat with foil and let stand for 10 minutes before carving. (The meats temperature will rise 5°F during standing.)

5 To serve, transfer meat to serving platter; remove strings from meat. If desired, garnish with peach wedges, Italian parsley, and rosemary. Carve meat into ¼- to ½-inch slices, being careful to keep the spiral intact.

Nutrition Facts per serving: 209 cal., 10 g total fat (3 g sat. fat), 69 mg chol., 342 mg sodium, 1 g carbo., 1 g fiber, 28 g pro.

sweet 'n' sticky CHICKEN

Prep: 30 minutes
Soak: 1 hour
Smoke: 1½ hours
Makes: 6 servings

- 6 to 8 maple or hickory wood chunks
- 6 whole chicken legs (drumstick and thigh)
- 1½ teaspoons dried oregano, crushed
- 1½ teaspoons dried thyme, crushed
- ½ teaspoon garlic salt
- ¼ teaspoon onion powder
- ¼ teaspoon black pepper
- Sweet 'n' Sticky Barbecue Sauce*

1 At least 1 hour before smoke cooking, soak wood chunks in enough water to cover. Drain before using.

2 If desired, remove skin from chicken. For rub, in a small bowl stir together oregano, thyme, garlic salt, onion powder, and pepper. Sprinkle evenly over chicken; rub in with your fingers.

3 In a smoker arrange preheated coals, drained wood chunks, and water pan according to the manufacturer's directions. Pour water into pan. Place chicken on the grill rack over water pan. Cover; smoke for 1½ to 2 hours or until chicken is tender and juices run clear (180°F). Add additional coals and water as needed to maintain temperature and moisture. Remove chicken from smoker.

4 Meanwhile, prepare Sweet 'N' Sticky Barbecue Sauce. Generously brush some of the warm sauce over smoked chicken. Pass remaining sauce.

***Sweet 'N' Sticky Barbecue Sauce:** In a small saucepan cook ½ cup finely chopped onion (1 medium) and 2 cloves garlic, minced, in 1 tablespoon hot olive oil until onion is tender. Stir in ¾ cup bottled chili sauce, ½ cup unsweetened pineapple juice, ¼ cup honey, 2 tablespoons Worcestershire sauce, and ½ teaspoon dry mustard. Bring to boiling; reduce heat. Simmer, uncovered, for 20 to 25 minutes or until desired consistency. Makes about 1¼ cups.

Nutrition Facts per serving: 535 cal., 29 g total fat (8 g sat. fat), 186 mg chol., 725 mg sodium, 25 g carbo., 2 g fiber, 43 g pro.

hickory-smoked TURKEY

Prep: 15 minutes
Soak: 1 hour
Smoke: 5 hours
Stand: 15 minutes
Makes: 12 to 14 servings

- 10 to 12 hickory wood chunks
- 1 10 to 12-pound turkey
- 2 tablespoons olive oil
- 1 teaspoon dried thyme, crushed
- 1 teaspoon dried sage, crushed
- ½ teaspoon salt
- ¼ teaspoon pepper

1 At least 1 hour before smoke cooking, soak wood chunks in enough water to cover.

2 Remove the neck and giblets from turkey. Rub skin of turkey with oil. Sprinkle inside and out with thyme, sage, salt, and pepper. Skewer the neck skin to the back. Twist wing tips under back. Tuck drumsticks under the band of skin across the tail or tie the legs to tail with 100-percent-cotton string. Insert a meat thermometer into the center of an inside thigh muscle without it touching bone.

3 Drain wood chunks. In a smoker arrange preheated coals, drained wood chunks, and the water pan according to the manufacturer's directions. Pour water into pan. Place turkey, breast side up, on grill rack over water pan. Cover and smoke about 5 hours or until meat thermometer registers 180°F to 185°F. Add more coals, wood chunks, and water as needed. Cut band of skin or string between drumsticks two-thirds of the way through cooking. Remove turkey from smoker. Cover with foil; let stand for 15 minutes before carving.

Nutrition Facts per serving: 277 cal., 14 g total fat (4 g sat. fat), 120 mg chol., 173 mg sodium, 0 g carbo., 0 g fiber, 35 g pro.

Tip: To moisten meats and add flavor during smoking, try spraying meats with fruit juices before smoking. This puts moisture back into the meat as it dries during cooking. Or, for a water smoker, try varying the liquid in the water pan. Fruit juices—orange, apple, white grape, or cranberry—are great with poultry. For pork, try cider or red wine vinegar. Beer mixed with half water is a good companion for beef ribs or roasts.

barbecued TURKEY TENDERLOINS

Tahini infuses purchased barbecue sauce with its rich, nutty flavor. Also known as sesame butter, look for Tahini at health food stores, Middle-Eastern food markets, and some supermarkets.

Prep: 15 minutes
Soak: 1 hour
Smoke: 1¼ hours
Makes: 4 servings

- 6 to 8 hickory or oak wood chunks
- ½ cup bottled hickory barbecue sauce
- 1 small fresh jalapeño pepper, seeded and finely chopped
- 1 tablespoon tahini (sesame butter)
- 4 tomatillos, husked and halved lengthwise, or ½ cup salsa verde
- 2 turkey breast tenderloins (about 1 pound)
- 4 French-style rolls, split and toasted
- Spinach leaves

1 At least 1 hour before smoke cooking, soak wood chunks in enough water to cover. Drain before using.

2 For sauce, in a small bowl combine barbecue sauce, jalapeño pepper, and tahini. Transfer half of the sauce to another bowl and reserve until ready to serve. If using tomatillos, thread them onto metal skewers. Set aside.

3 In a smoker arrange preheated coals, drained wood chunks, and water pan according to the manufacturer's directions. Pour water into pan. Brush both sides of turkey with the remaining sauce. Place turkey on the grill rack over water pan. Cover; smoke for 1¼ to 1½ hours or until turkey is tender and juices run clear (170°F). Place tomatillos next to turkey on grill rack directly over coals during the last 20 minutes of cooking. Add additional coals and water as needed to maintain temperature and moisture. Remove turkey and tomatillos from smoker. Thinly slice the turkey and chop the tomatillos.

4 To serve, in a small saucepan cook and stir the reserved sauce over low heat until heated through. Remove from heat. Fill the toasted rolls with a few spinach leaves, the smoked turkey, and tomatillos or salsa verde. Top with the reserved sauce.

Nutrition Facts per serving: 303 cal., 5 g total fat (1 g sat. fat), 68 mg chol., 695 mg sodium, 32 g carbo., 1 g fiber, 31 g pro.

chili-rubbed DRUMSTICKS

Wisps of smoke and hot-and-spicy seasonings give turkey legs a bonanza of lip-tingling flavor.

Prep: 5 minutes
Soak: 1 hour
Smoke: 2½ hours
Makes: 6 servings

- 6 to 8 hickory wood chunks
- 1 tablespoon chili powder
- 1 tablespoon finely shredded lime peel
- 1½ teaspoons ground cumin
- ½ teaspoon salt
- 6 turkey drumsticks (about 3 to 4½ pounds)
- Bottled salsa or barbecue sauce (optional)

1 At least 1 hour before smoke cooking, soak wood chunks in enough water to cover. Drain before using.

2 For rub, in a small bowl combine chili powder, lime peel, cumin, and salt. Sprinkle mixture evenly over turkey; rub in with your fingers.

3 In a smoker arrange preheated coals, drained wood chunks, and water pan according to the manufacturers directions. Pour water into pan. Place drumsticks on grill rack over water. Cover; smoke for 2½ to 3 hours or until turkey is tender and juice runs clear (180°F). Add additional coals and water as needed to maintain temperature and moisture. If desired, serve the turkey with salsa.

Nutrition Facts per serving: 178 cal., 9 g total fat (3 g sat. fat), 80 mg chol., 269 mg sodium, 1 g carbo., 1 g fiber, 22 g pro.

honey SMOKED TROUT

Smoking adds another dimension to trout, and the cream sauce makes the finished fish magnificent.

Prep: 10 minutes
Soak: 1 hour
Smoke: 1½ hours
Marinate: 2 hours
Makes: 4 servings

- 4 8- to 10-ounce fresh or frozen dressed, boned rainbow trout
- ¼ teaspoon salt
- ¼ teaspoon ground white pepper
- 3 tablespoons honey
- 2 tablespoons orange juice
- 4 hickory or apple wood chunks
- ⅓ cup whipping cream
- 2 tablespoons lemon juice
- 1 tablespoon prepared horseradish
- Salt and white pepper
- Fresh dill sprigs

1 Thaw fish, if frozen. Rinse fish; pat dry. In a large shallow dish spread the fish open, skin sides down and overlapping as necessary. Sprinkle with salt and white pepper. In a small bowl stir together the honey and orange juice; spoon evenly over the fish. Cover and marinate in the refrigerator for 2 hours.

2 At least 1 hour before smoke-cooking, soak wood chunks in enough water to cover.

3 Meanwhile, for sauce, in a medium bowl beat the whipping cream just until it starts to thicken. Stir in the lemon juice and horseradish. Season to taste with additional salt and white pepper. Cover and chill until ready to serve.

4 Drain wood chunks. In a smoker arrange preheated coals, drained wood chunks, and water pan according to the manufacturer's directions. Pour water into pan. Fold the fish closed and place on grill rack over water pan. Cover and smoke for 1½ to 2 hours or until fish flakes easily when tested with a fork. Add more coals, wood chunks, and water as needed.

5 Serve fish with the sauce. Garnish with dill sprigs.

Nutrition Facts per serving: 395 cal., 15 g total fat (6 g sat. fat), 157 mg chol., 277 mg sodium, 15 g carbo., 0 g fiber, 47 g pro.

double-smoked SALMON WITH HORSERADISH CREAM

This fresh salmon dish is twice as nice because it's fresh salmon stuffed with smoked salmon and then smoked in a smoker.

Prep: 15 minutes
Soak: 1 hour
Smoke: 30 minutes
Makes: 4 servings

- 4 hickory or apple wood chunks
- 4 6-ounce fresh or frozen salmon fillets (with skin), about 1 inch thick
- 4 slices smoked salmon (about 3 ounces)
- 4 teaspoons snipped fresh dill
- 1 tablespoon lemon juice
  Salt
  Black pepper
  Horseradish Cream*

1 At least 1 hour before smoke cooking, soak wood chunks in enough water to cover. Drain before using.

2 Thaw salmon fillets, if frozen. Rinse fillets; pat dry with paper towels. Make a pocket in each fish fillet by cutting horizontally from one side almost to but not through the other side. Fill with smoked salmon slices and 2 teaspoons of the dill, folding salmon slices as necessary to fit. Brush fish with lemon juice and top with the remaining 2 teaspoons of the dill. Sprinkle with salt and pepper.

3 In a smoker arrange preheated coals, drained wood chunks, and water pan according to the manufacturer's directions. Pour water into pan. Place fish, skin sides down, on grill rack over water pan. Cover; smoke about 30 minutes or until fish flakes easily when tested with a fork. Serve fish with Horseradish Cream.

*Horseradish Cream: In a small bowl stir together ½ cup dairy sour cream, 2 tablespoons thinly sliced green onion (1), 4 teaspoons prepared horseradish, and 2 teaspoons snipped fresh dill. Makes about ⅔ cup.

Nutrition Facts per serving: 245 cal., 13 g total fat (5 g sat. fat), 48 mg chol., 337 mg sodium, 2 g carbo., 0 g fiber, 29 g pro.

tropical halibut STEAKS

Toasting the coconut for this tropically inclined entrée heightens its sweet nuttiness. Simply bake the coconut in a 350°F oven about 10 minutes, stirring once, until its golden.

Prep: 15 minutes
Soak: 1 hour
Marinate: 1 hour
Smoke: 45 minutes
Makes: 4 servings

- 4 apple or orange wood chunks
- 4 6-ounce fresh or frozen halibut steaks, cut 1 inch thick
- ⅓ cup pineapple-orange juice
- ⅓ cup soy sauce
- ¼ teaspoon curry powder
- Chunky Pineapple Sauce*
- 2 tablespoons coconut, toasted

1 At least 1 hour before smoke cooking, soak wood chunks in enough water to cover. Drain before using.

2 Thaw fish, if frozen. Rinse fish; pat dry with paper towels. Place fish in a resealable plastic bag set in a shallow dish. For marinade, in a small bowl combine pineapple-orange juice, soy sauce, and curry powder. Pour marinade over fish; seal bag. Marinate in the refrigerator for 1 hour, turning bag occasionally.

3 Drain fish, reserving marinade. In a smoker arrange preheated coals, drained wood chunks, and water pan according to the manufacturers directions. Pour water into pan. Place fish on the greased grill rack over water pan. Cover; smoke for 45 to 60 minutes or until fish flakes easily when tested with a fork, brushing once with marinade halfway through cooking. Discard the remaining marinade.

4 To serve, if necessary, reheat the Chunky Pineapple Sauce and spoon over fish. Sprinkle the fish with toasted coconut.

***Chunky Pineapple Sauce:** Drain one 8-ounce can pineapple chunks (juice pack), reserving juice. Peel and seed ¼ of a medium cantaloupe or ½ of a papaya. Finely chop pineapple and cantaloupe or papaya. In a small saucepan combine the chopped fruit and a dash curry powder. Add enough water to the reserved pineapple juice to make ½ cup liquid. Stir in 2 teaspoons cornstarch; add to the fruit mixture. Cook and stir over medium heat until thickened and bubbly. Cook and stir for 2 minutes more. Remove from heat.

Nutrition Facts per serving: 262 cal., 5 g total fat (1 g sat. fat), 54 mg chol., 740 mg sodium, 16 g carbo., 1 g fiber, 38 g pro.

on
THE SIDE

Grilled Potato Salad, *page 209*

tomato-squash SALAD

Cubed zucchini or yellow summer squash makes a good substitute if baby squash aren't available.

Prep: 15 minutes
Cook: 5 minutes
Cool: 10 minutes
Makes: 8 servings

- 8 ounces baby pattypan squash and/or baby zucchini (about 2 cups)
- 4 cups red and/or yellow currant tomatoes
- 1 to 2 cups fresh arugula or romaine lettuce, coarsely torn
- 2 tablespoons snipped fresh basil, tarragon, and/or chives
- ¼ cup olive oil
- ¼ cup red wine vinegar or champagne vinegar
- 1 tablespoon lime juice or lemon juice
- ¼ teaspoon salt
- ⅛ teaspoon ground black pepper

1 In a large saucepan cook squash, covered, in enough lightly salted boiling water to cover about 5 minutes or until tender. Drain. Cool squash by adding cold water and ice cubes to pan. Drain well.

2 In a serving bowl combine the drained squash, tomatoes, arugula, and herbs.

3 For dressing in a screw-top jar combine oil, vinegar, lime juice, salt, and pepper. Cover and shake well. Add half of the dressing to the vegetables; toss to coat. Season to taste with additional salt and pepper. Serve remaining dressing.

Nutrition Facts per serving: 82 cal., 7 g total fat (1 g sat. fat), 0 mg chol., 57 mg sodium, 5 g carbo., 2 g fiber, 1 g pro.

basil-cucumber SALAD

Prep: 10 minutes
Stand: 15 minutes
Makes: 5 servings

- 2 medium cucumbers, peeled
- 3 tablespoons rice vinegar
- 2 teaspoons sugar
- ½ teaspoon salt
- ½ teaspoon finely shredded lime peel
- ½ teaspoon grated fresh ginger
- ¼ teaspoon crushed red pepper
- 2 tablespoons thinly sliced fresh basil

1 Using a vegetable peeler peel thin strips of peel from cucumbers. Halve cucumbers lengthwise. Seed and slice crosswise into ¼-inch-thick slices.

2 In a medium bowl combine cucumbers, rice vinegar, sugar, salt, lime peel, ginger, and crushed red pepper. Toss to mix. Let stand for 15 minutes. Stir in basil. Serve with a slotted spoon.

Nutrition Facts per serving: 30 cal., 0 g total fat (0 g sat. fat), 0 mg chol., 235 mg sodium, 7 g carbo., 1 g fiber, 0 g pro.

grilled potato SALAD

If you like the tangy sweetness of German-style potato salad, you'll love this grilled version. A maple-mustard vinaigrette dresses chopped potatoes, crumbled bacon, and hard-cooked eggs.

Prep: 25 minutes
Grill: 50 minutes
Makes: 8 to 10 side-dish servings

- 6 medium Yukon gold potatoes (about 2 pounds)
- 1 tablespoon olive oil
- ⅓ cup white balsamic vinegar
- ⅓ cup olive oil
- 1 tablespoon snipped fresh sage
- 1 tablespoon Dijon-style mustard
- 1 teaspoon maple syrup
- 1 clove garlic, minced
- ¼ teaspoon salt
- ⅛ teaspoon black pepper
- 2 cups fresh baby spinach
- 4 slices bacon, crisp-cooked, drained, and crumbled
- 2 hard-cooked eggs, coarsely chopped
- ¼ cup finely chopped red onion

1 Scrub potatoes thoroughly with a brush; pat dry. Prick potatoes with a fork. Rub potatoes with the 1 tablespoon olive oil.

2 For a charcoal grill, arrange medium-hot coals around edge of grill. Test for medium heat above center of grill. Place potatoes on grill rack over center of grill. Cover; grill for 50 to 60 minutes or until potatoes are tender. (For a gas grill, preheat grill. Reduce heat to medium. Adjust for indirect cooking. Grill as above.)

3 Meanwhile, for vinaigrette, in a screw-top jar combine vinegar, the ⅓ cup olive oil, the sage, mustard, maple syrup, garlic, salt, and pepper. Cover and shake well. Set aside.

4 When potatoes are done, remove from grill and cool slightly. Coarsely chop potatoes. Transfer potatoes to an extra large bowl. Stir in spinach, bacon, eggs, and red onion. Gently stir in vinaigrette until combined.

Nutrition Facts per serving: 221 cal., 14 g total fat (3 g sat. fat), 56 mg chol., 209 mg sodium, 19 g carbo., 2 g fiber, 5 g pro.

two-tone COLESLAW

If you plan to chill this salad for more than two hours, toss the apple slices in a little lemon juice to keep them crisp and fresh-looking.

Prep: 20 minutes
Chill: 2 hours
Makes: 12 side-dish servings

- ⅔ cup light mayonnaise
- 3 tablespoons cider vinegar
- 1 tablespoon snipped fresh dill or 1 teaspoon dried dillweed
- ½ teaspoon salt
- ½ teaspoon coarsely ground black pepper
- 7 cups shredded green cabbage
- 3 medium apples, cored and thinly sliced
- 1 cup chopped sweet onions
- Fresh dill sprig (optional)

1 For dressing, in an extra-large bowl stir together mayonnaise, vinegar, snipped dill, salt, and pepper. Stir in cabbage, apples, and onions. Cover and chill at least 2 hours or up to 48 hours, stirring occasionally. If desired, garnish with fresh dill.

Nutrition Facts per serving: 78 cal., 5 g total fat (1 g sat. fat), 5 mg chol., 195 mg sodium, 10 g carbo., 2 g fiber, 1 g pro.

honey-mustard SLAW

Prep: 25 minutes
Chill: 2 to 8 hours
Makes: 8 servings

- 8 cups shredded red and/or green cabbage (about 1 head)
- 2 cups snow pea pods or sugar snap pea pods, halved crosswise
- 2 medium carrots, shredded
- ½ cup chopped red onion
- ⅓ cup coarse-grain brown mustard
- ¼ cup lemon juice
- ¼ cup salad oil
- ¼ cup honey
- 2 cloves garlic, minced
- 3 tablespoons chopped nuts

1 In a very large bowl combine cabbage, pea pods, carrots, and red onion; toss gently to combine. For dressing: In a screw-top jar combine mustard, lemon juice, oil, honey, and garlic. Cover and shake well.

2 Pour dressing over cabbage mixture; toss gently to coat. Cover and chill for 2 to 8 hours. Before serving, stir cabbage mixture. Sprinkle with nuts.

Nutrition Facts per serving: 168 cal., 9 g total fat (1 g sat. fat), 0 mg chol., 273 mg sodium, 19 g carbo., 3 g fiber, 2 g pro.

grilled PANZANELLA

Prep: 20 minutes
Grill: 20 minutes
Stand: 30 minutes
Makes: 12 side-dish servings

- 8 ounces crusty country bread, sliced 1 inch thick
- 2 medium yellow, red, and/or green sweet peppers, seeded and quartered lengthwise
- 1 medium red onion, sliced ½ inch thick
- 2 tablespoons olive oil
- 3 large tomatoes, coarsely chopped
- 1 medium cucumber, coarsely chopped
- 3 tablespoons drained capers (optional)
- 2 tablespoons olive oil
- 1 tablespoon red wine vinegar
- ¼ teaspoon salt
- ¼ teaspoon ground black pepper

1 Brush bread slices, sweet peppers, and onion with 2 tablespoons oil. For a charcoal grill, place bread and vegetables on the rack of an uncovered grill directly over medium coals. Grill bread slices for 2 to 4 minutes or until browned, turning once halfway through grilling. Grill sweet peppers for 20 minutes, turning once halfway through grilling. Grill onion for 10 to 15 minutes or until crisp-tender, turning once halfway through grilling. (For a gas grill, preheat grill. Reduce heat to medium. Place bread and vegetables on grill rack over heat. Cover and grill as directed above.)

2 Cut bread and sweet peppers into 1-inch pieces. Coarsely chop onion. In a large serving bowl combine bread, sweet peppers, onion, tomatoes, cucumber, and, if desired, capers.

3 For dressing, in a small bowl combine 2 tablespoons oil, the vinegar, salt, and black pepper. Drizzle over vegetable mixture; toss gently to coat. Let stand at room temperature for 30 minutes before serving.

Nutrition Facts per serving: 113 cal., 5 g total fat (1 g sat. fat), 0 mg chol., 175 mg sodium, 15 g carbo., 2 g fiber, 5 g pro.

corn SALAD

Start to Finish: 25 minutes
Makes: 9 (⅔-cup) servings

- ¼ cup lime juice
- 1 tablespoon honey
- 1 fresh jalapeño chile pepper, seeded and finely chopped*
- 3 tablespoons snipped fresh cilantro or 1 tablespoon snipped fresh mint
- ¼ teaspoon salt
- 6 fresh ears of sweet corn
- 1½ cups fresh baby spinach
- 1 large tomato, seeded and chopped
- ¾ cup seeded and chopped cucumber
- Small fresh peppers (optional)

1 For dressing, in a large nonreactive bowl whisk together lime juice and honey until well combined. Stir in jalapeño pepper, cilantro, and salt.

2 Using a sharp knife, carefully cut corn kernels off the cobs. Add corn to dressing in bowl. Stir in spinach, tomato, and cucumber. Serve immediately or cover and chill for up to 1 hour. If desired, garnish with whole peppers.

Nutrition Facts per serving: 59 cal., 1 g fat (0 g sat. fat) 0 mg chol., 78 mg sodium, 13 g carbo., 2 g fiber, 2 g pro.

***Note:** Because hot chile peppers, such as jalapeños, contain volatile oils that can burn your skin and eyes, avoid direct contact with chiles as much as possible. When working with chile peppers, wear plastic or rubber gloves. If your bare hands do touch the chile peppers, wash your hands well with soap and water.

summer vegetable PASTA SALAD

To make enough salad for more than one meal, double the ingredient amounts and cut preparation time needed for another meal.

Prep: 30 minutes
Makes: 4 to 6 servings

- 8 ounces dried campanelle, penne, or mostaccioli pasta (2⅓ cups)
- 1 tablespoon extra virgin olive oil
- 6 to 8 cloves garlic, thinly sliced
- 1 medium zucchini (8 ounces), trimmed and cut into matchstick-size strips (2 cups)
- 8 ounces sugar snap peas, strings removed
- 2 cups cherry or grape tomatoes, halved
- 3 tablespoons finely chopped shallot (1)
- 1 tablespoon sherry vinegar or white wine vinegar
- 1 tablespoon Dijon-style mustard
- ½ teaspoon salt
- ¼ teaspoon ground black pepper
- ¼ cup extra virgin olive oil
- 3 tablespoons chopped fresh parsley
- Finely shredded Asiago cheese (optional)

1 Bring a large pot of lightly salted water to boiling; add pasta and cook according to package directions. Drain and rinse pasta under cold water; drain again. Transfer pasta to a large bowl.

2 In a large nonstick skillet heat 1 tablespoon oil over medium-high heat. Add garlic; cook and stir for 30 seconds. Add zucchini; cook and stir for 1 minute. Add snap peas; cook and stir 30 seconds. Stir in tomatoes; cook about 30 seconds or until tomatoes begin to soften. Transfer vegetable mixture to pasta bowl; toss to mix.

3 For shallot-mustard dressing, in a small bowl combine shallot, vinegar, mustard, salt, and pepper. Slowly whisk in ¼ cup oil; stir in parsley. Pour dressing over pasta mixture, tossing to coat. Serve immediately or cover and chill for 4 hours or up to 3 days to allow flavors to meld. Before serving, sprinkle each serving with Asiago cheese.

Nutrition Facts per serving: 434 cal., 18 g total fat (2 g sat. fat), 0 mg chol., 404 mg sodium, 57 g carbo., 5 g fiber, 12 g pro.

summer STRAWBERRY SALAD

Hold back on adding the banana if you opt to chill the greens mixture. Add the bananas, freshly peeled and sliced, when you toss the salad with the dressing.

Start to Finish: 20 minutes
Makes: 6 to 8 servings

- 6 cups chopped romaine lettuce
- 3 cups sliced fresh strawberries
- 2 cups cubed fresh pineapple
- 1 banana, sliced
- ¼ cup water
- ¼ cup cream of coconut
- 2 tablespoons lemon juice
- 1 tablespoon yellow mustard
- ½ teaspoon ground ginger
- ¼ cup sliced almonds, toasted (optional)

1 In an extra-large bowl toss together romaine, strawberries, pineapple, and banana. If desired, cover and chill for up to 1 hour.

2 For dressing, in a small bowl whisk together the water, cream of coconut, lemon juice, mustard, and ginger. If desired, cover and chill until ready to serve.

3 To serve, drizzle dressing over greens mixture; toss gently to coat. If desired, sprinkle with almonds.

Nutrition Facts per serving: 111 cal., 4 g total fat (3 g sat. fat), 0 mg chol., 35 mg sodium, 20 g carbo., 4 g fiber, 2 g pro.

zucchini PANCAKES

These golden dinnertime treats, flavored with Parmesan cheese and onion, make great party appetizers, too.

Prep: 20 minutes
Cook: 4 minutes per batch
Stand: 15 minutes
Makes: about 30 pancakes

- 4 to 5 medium zucchini (about 1½ pounds)
- ¾ teaspoon salt
- 4 eggs
- 1 clove garlic, minced
- ¾ cup all-purpose flour
- ½ cup grated Parmesan cheese
- 1 tablespoon finely chopped onion
- ¼ teaspoon ground black pepper
- Dairy sour cream (optional)

1 Trim and coarsely shred zucchini (you should have about 5 cups). In a large bowl toss zucchini with salt. Place zucchini in a colander. Place a plate or 9-inch pie plate on top of zucchini; weight down with cans. Let drain for 15 minutes. Discard liquid.

2 Preheat oven to 300°F. In the large bowl beat together eggs and garlic. Stir in flour, Parmesan cheese, onion, and pepper until just moistened (batter should be lumpy). Stir in zucchini until just combined.

3 For each zucchini pancake, spoon 1 heaping tablespoon batter onto a hot, lightly oiled griddle or heavy skillet, spreading to form a 3-inch circle. Cook over medium heat for 2 to 3 minutes on each side or until the pancake is golden brown. (Reduce heat to medium-low if pancakes brown too quickly.) Keep pancakes warm in the preheated oven while cooking remaining pancakes.

4 If desired, serve pancakes topped with a spoonful of sour cream.

Nutrition Facts per serving: 31 cal., 1 g total fat (0 g sat. fat), 29 mg chol., 90 mg sodium, 3 g carbo., 0 g fiber, 2 g pro.

Make Ahead: Prepare and cook pancakes as directed. Cool completely. Place pancakes in a freezer container, separating layers with waxed paper; cover. Freeze for up to 3 months. To reheat, preheat oven to 425°F. Place frozen pancakes in a single layer on a greased baking sheet. Bake, uncovered, for 8 to 10 minutes or until hot and slightly crisp.

mexicali VEGETABLE KABOBS

Chili powder and cumin tint the corn and zucchini a lovely auburn color. When assembling the kabobs push the skewers through the soft centers of the cobs.

Prep: 30 minutes
Grill: 15 minutes
Makes: 6 side-dish servings

- 4 ears fresh corn, cut into 2-inch pieces
- 2 medium zucchini and/or yellow summer squash, cut into 1-inch slices
- 1 red onion, cut into wedges
- ⅓ cup butter or margarine, melted
- 1 teaspoon chili powder
- ½ teaspoon ground cumin
- ¼ teaspoon garlic powder
- ¼ teaspoon dried oregano, crushed

1 On six 12-inch skewers alternately thread the corn, zucchini, and onion wedges. In a small bowl combine the butter, chili powder, cumin, garlic powder, and oregano. Brush over vegetables.

2 For a charcoal grill, grill kabobs on the rack of an uncovered grill directly over medium coals for 15 to 18 minutes or until vegetables are tender and brown, turning and brushing occasionally with butter mixture. (For a gas grill, preheat grill. Reduce heat to medium. Place kabobs on grill rack over heat. Cover and grill as above.)

Nutrition Facts per serving: 160 cal., 12 g total fat (7 g sat. fat), 29 mg chol., 124 mg sodium, 14 g carbo., 3 g fiber, 3 g pro.

aloha KABOBS

These pretty skewers lend a Hawaiian air to any meal that features grilled fish, pork, or poultry. If you can't find red pearl onions, the white ones will do.

Prep: 30 minutes
Grill: 6 minutes
Makes: 10 side-dish servings

- 10 8-inch wooden skewers
- 1 fresh pineapple, peeled, cored, and cut into 1-inch pieces (about 3 cups)
- 20 red pearl onions, peeled
- 2 yellow and/or red sweet peppers, cut into 1-inch pieces
- 20 sugar snap peas
- ¼ cup purchased teriyaki or Szechwan glaze

1 Soak the wooden skewers in water for 30 minutes. Drain. Alternately thread pineapple, onions, peppers, and peas onto skewers, leaving a ¼-inch space between pieces.

2 For a charcoal grill, grill kabobs on the rack of an uncovered grill, directly over medium coals for 6 to 8 minutes or just until onions are tender and pineapple is heated through, turning once halfway through grilling and brushing frequently with glaze. (For a gas grill, preheat grill. Reduce to medium heat. Place kabobs on grill rack over heat. Cover and grill as above).

Nutrition Facts per serving: 59 cal., 0 g total fat (0 g sat. fat), 0 mg chol., 250 mg sodium, 13 g carbo., 2 g fiber, 2 g pro.

grilled corn WITH CUMIN-LIME BUTTER

Prep: 30 minutes
Grill: 25 minutes
Stand: 1 hour
Makes: 6 servings

- 6 fresh ears of sweet corn with husks
- 2 quarts cold tap water
- 1 tablespoon coarse (kosher) salt
- Cumin-Lime Butter*

1 Carefully peel the cornhusks down to the bottom of each ear without detaching. Remove and discard the silks. Gently rinse the corn. Carefully fold husks back around ears. Tie husks tops with 100%-cotton kitchen string to secure.

2 In an extra-large bowl or tub combine the cold water and salt, stirring until salt mostly dissolves. Place corn in the water. Put a pan on top of corn to keep all ears submerged for 1 hour before grilling. Drain corn; pat dry.

3 Place corn on the grill rack directly over medium coals. Grill, covered, for 25 to 30 minutes or until kernels are tender, turning and rearranging with long-handled tongs three times.

4 To serve, remove string from corn; discard string. Peel back husks. Serve corn with Cumin-Lime Butter.

*Cumin-Lime Butter: In a small cast-iron or heavy skillet cook and stir 1 tablespoon cumin seeds over low heat for 1 minute. Add 1 teaspoon coarse (kosher) salt and ¼ teaspoon ground chipotle chile pepper. Cook and stir about 1 minute more or until seeds become fragrant and lightly colored. Remove from heat; shake skillet for 1 minute. Place cumin mixture in a spice or coffee grinder. Cover and pulse until ground. In a small bowl stir together 1 cup butter, softened; cumin mixture; and 2 teaspoons finely shredded lime peel. Serve on grilled sweet corn. Refrigerate any remaining butter in tightly covered container for up to 3 days.

Nutrition Facts per ear of corn with 1 tablespoon butter: 353 cal., 32 g total fat (20 g sat. fat), 81 mg chol., 877 mg sodium, 18 g carbo., 3 g fiber, 3 g pro.

ranch-style CARROTS AND SQUASH

Ranch salad dressing makes an easy, tasty sauce for this mixed veggie packet.

Prep: 20 minutes
Grill: 20 minutes
Makes: 4 side-dish servings

- 2½ cups packaged peeled baby carrots (about 14 ounces)
- 2 cups baby sunburst squash, green baby pattypans, or 1 medium zucchini or yellow summer squash, cut into ½-inch slices
- 1 cup grape tomatoes
- ½ cup bottled ranch salad dressing
- 2 teaspoons all-purpose flour
- 1 teaspoon finely shredded lemon peel
- ¼ cup fine dry bread crumbs
- ¼ cup finely chopped walnuts, toasted
- 2 tablespoons finely shredded Parmesan cheese
- 1 tablespoon olive oil

1 In a medium saucepan cook carrots in a small amount of boiling salted water for 5 minutes; drain.

2 Cut any large baby squash in half. In a large bowl combine drained carrots, squash, and tomatoes. In a small bowl combine salad dressing, flour, and lemon peel; stir into vegetable mixture. Tear off a 36x18-inch piece of heavy-duty foil; fold in half to make an 18-inch square. Place the vegetables in the center of foil. Bring up two opposite edges of foil and seal with a double fold. Fold remaining edges together to completely enclose vegetables, leaving space for steam to build.

3 For a charcoal grill, grill vegetable packet on the rack of an uncovered grill directly over medium coals for 20 to 25 minutes or until carrots are tender, turning packet once halfway through grilling. (For a gas grill, preheat grill. Reduce heat to medium. Place vegetables on grill rack over heat. Cover and grill as above.)

4 Meanwhile, in another small bowl combine bread crumbs, walnuts, Parmesan cheese, and oil. Carefully open packet (mixture may appear slightly curdled). Sprinkle with crumb mixture.

Nutrition Facts per serving: 384 cal., 30 g total fat (6 g sat. fat), 17 mg chol., 736 mg sodium, 21 g carbo., 2 g fiber, 10 g pro.

fire-roasted ACORN SQUASH

Instead of the usual glaze of brown sugar and butter, try basting rings of squash with tarragon butter. They're delicious served with pork and a dry white wine.

Prep: 10 minutes
Grill: 45 minutes
Makes: 4 side-dish servings

- 1 tablespoon olive oil
- ½ teaspoon salt
- ¼ teaspoon black pepper
- 2 small acorn squash, cut crosswise into 1-inch rings and seeded
- 2 tablespoons butter or margarine, melted
- 2 teaspoons snipped fresh tarragon or ½ teaspoon dried tarragon, crushed

1 In a small bowl combine oil, salt, and pepper; brush over squash rings. In another small bowl stir together melted butter and tarragon; set aside.

2 For a charcoal grill, arrange medium-hot coals around a drip pan. Test for medium heat above the pan. Place squash rings on grill rack over drip pan. Cover; grill about 45 minutes or until squash is tender, turning squash occasionally and brushing with butter mixture after 30 minutes of grilling. (For a gas grill, preheat grill. Reduce heat to medium. Adjust for indirect cooking. Grill as above.)

Nutrition Facts per serving: 153 cal., 10 g total fat (4 g sat. fat), 16 mg chol., 358 mg sodium, 18 g carbo., 3 g fiber, 1 g pro.

grilled asparagus IN DILL BUTTER

To prevent flare-ups, grill the buttery asparagus spears in a disposable foil pan. The pan prevents the butter from dripping into the fire.

Prep: 10 minutes
Grill: 7 minutes
Makes: 4 to 6 side-dish servings

- 1 pound asparagus spears, trimmed
- 2 tablespoons butter, melted
- 1 tablespoon snipped fresh dill or 1 teaspoon dried dill
- 1 clove garlic, minced
- ¼ teaspoon cracked black pepper
- Finely shredded Parmesan cheese

1 Place asparagus in a large disposable foil pan. Drizzle with butter and sprinkle with dill, garlic, and pepper. Toss to mix.

2 For a charcoal grill, place foil pan on the rack of an uncovered grill directly over medium coals. Grill for 7 to 10 minutes or until asparagus is crisp-tender, stirring occasionally. (For a gas grill, preheat grill. Reduce heat to medium. Place foil pan on grill rack over heat. Cover and grill as above.)

3 To serve, transfer asparagus to a serving dish. Sprinkle with Parmesan cheese.

Nutrition Facts per serving: 142 cal., 11 g total fat (7 g sat. fat), 28 mg chol., 355 mg sodium, 2 g carbo., 1 g fiber, 8 g pro.

cheesy garlic POTATO GRATIN

Medium-starch potatoes such as Yukon gold and Finnish Yellow contain more moisture than high-starch potatoes such as russets. They're a good choice for gratins and casseroles because they retain their shape after cooking.

Prep: 15 minutes
Bake: 1¼ hours
Oven: 350°F
Makes: 6 to 8 side-dish servings

- 1½ pounds Yukon gold or other yellow potatoes, thinly sliced (about 5 cups)
- ⅓ cup sliced green onions
- 1½ cups shredded Swiss cheese (6 ounces)
- 4 cloves garlic, minced
- 1 teaspoon salt
- ¼ teaspoon black pepper
- 1 cup whipping cream

1 Grease a 2-quart square baking dish. Layer half of the sliced potatoes and half of the green onions in the dish. Sprinkle with half of the Swiss cheese, garlic, salt, and pepper. Repeat layers. Pour whipping cream over top.

2 Bake, covered, in a 350°F oven for 1 hour. Uncover and bake for 15 to 20 minutes more or until potatoes are tender and top is golden brown.

Nutrition Facts per serving: 365 cal., 23 g total fat (14 g sat. fat), 80 mg chol., 454 mg sodium, 30 g carbo., 1 g fiber, 12 g pro.

grilled cheesy POTATOES

These camp-style potatoes, grilled in a foil pouch, are sure to be a family favorite.

Prep: 25 minutes
Grill: 30 minutes
Makes: 4 servings

- **Nonstick cooking spray**
- 1½ pounds small red potatoes, cut into thin wedges
- 1 cup chopped red onion (1 large)
- 6 cloves garlic
- ¼ to ½ teaspoon salt
- ¼ teaspoon ground black pepper
- ¼ cup butter, cut into 1-inch pieces
- ½ cup shredded Swiss cheese (2 ounces)
- ¼ cup grated Parmesan cheese

1 Fold a 36x18-inch piece of heavy-duty foil in half to make an 18-inch square. Lightly coat the foil with cooking spray. Place potatoes, onion, and garlic in center of foil. Sprinkle with garlic powder, salt, and black pepper. Top with butter pieces, Swiss cheese, and Parmesan cheese. Bring up opposite sides of foil and seal with a double fold. Fold remaining edges together to completely enclose vegetables, leaving space for steam to build.

2 For a charcoal grill, place vegetable packet on the grill rack directly over medium coals. Grill, uncovered, for 30 to 35 minutes or until potatoes are tender, turning packet over once. (For a gas grill, preheat grill. Reduce heat to medium. Place vegetables on the grill rack over heat. Cover and grill as above.) Serve immediately.

Nutrition Facts per serving: 326 cal., 18 g total fat (10 g sat. fat), 50 mg chol., 348 mg sodium, 33 g carbo., 4 g fiber, 10 g pro.

moroccan-style CARROTS

The microwave oven makes quick work of these tangy marinated carrots. Their Mediterranean flavor goes especially well with grilled lamb chops or beef steaks.

Prep: 10 minutes
Microwave: 6 minutes
Stand: 1 hour
Makes: 6 servings

- 1 pound carrots, bias-cut into ½-inch-thick slices
- 2 tablespoons water
- 1 tablespoon olive oil
- 1 tablespoon cider vinegar
- ½ to ¾ teaspoon ground cumin
- ½ teaspoon kosher salt or ¼ teaspoon salt
- ¼ teaspoon ground coriander
- Dash cayenne pepper
- 1 cup sliced sweet onion (such as Vidalia, Maui, or Walla Walla)
- ¼ cup snipped fresh cilantro

1 In a large microwave-safe bowl combine carrot slices and the water. Cover and microwave on 100% power (high) for 6 to 9 minutes or until crisp-tender, stirring once. Transfer carrots to a bowl filled with ice water. Let stand for 5 minutes. Drain and pat carrots dry with a paper towel.

2 In the same large bowl combine oil, vinegar, cumin, salt, coriander, and cayenne pepper. Stir in carrots, sweet onion, and cilantro; toss to combine. Let stand at room temperature for 1 hour before serving.

Nutrition Facts per serving: 58 cal., 2 g total fat (0 g sat. fat), 0 mg chol., 212 mg sodium, 9 g carbo., 2 g fiber, 1 g pro.

Make Ahead: Prepare as directed through Step 2, excluding the standing time. Cover and refrigerate for up to 24 hours. Let stand at room temperature for 1 hour before serving.

baked bean QUINTET

Make this crowd-pleasing favorite for your next backyard barbecue—it's a classic that can't miss.

Prep: 10 minutes
Bake: 1 hour
Oven: 375°F
Makes: 12 to 16 side-dish servings

- 6 slices bacon, cut up
- 1 cup chopped onion (1 large)
- 1 clove garlic, minced
- 1 16-ounce can lima beans, drained
- 1 16-ounce can pork and beans in tomato sauce
- 1 15½-ounce can red kidney beans, rinsed and drained
- 1 15-ounce can garbanzo beans (chickpeas), rinsed and drained
- 1 15-ounce can butter beans, drained
- ¾ cup ketchup
- ½ cup molasses
- ¼ cup packed brown sugar
- 1 tablespoon prepared mustard
- 1 tablespoon Worcestershire sauce
- Crumbled, cooked bacon (optional)

1 In a skillet cook the cut-up bacon, onion, and garlic until bacon is crisp and onion is tender; drain. In a bowl combine onion mixture, lima beans, pork and beans, kidney beans, garbanzo beans, butter beans, ketchup, molasses, brown sugar, mustard, and Worcestershire sauce. Transfer bean mixture to a 3-quart casserole.

2 Bake, covered, in a 375°F oven for 1 hour. If desired, top with additional cooked bacon.

Nutrition Facts per serving: 245 cal., 3 g total fat (1 g sat. fat), 5 mg chol., 882 mg sodium, 47 g carbo., 9 g fiber, 10 g pro.

Slow cooker directions: Prepare bean mixture as above. Transfer to a 3½- or 4-quart slow cooker. Cover and cook on low-heat setting for 10 to 12 hours or on high-heat setting for 4 to 5 hours.

233

metric information

The charts on this page provide a guide for converting measurements from the U.S. customary system, which is used throughout this book, to the metric system.

PRODUCT DIFFERENCES

Most of the ingredients called for in the recipes in this book are available in most countries. However, some are known by different names. Here are some common American ingredients and their possible counterparts:

- Sugar (white) is granulated, fine granulated, or castor sugar.
- Powdered sugar is icing sugar.
- All-purpose flour is enriched, bleached, or unbleached white household flour. When self-rising flour is used in place of all-purpose flour in a recipe that calls for leavening, omit the leavening agent (baking soda or baking powder) and salt.
- Light-color corn syrup is golden syrup.
- Cornstarch is cornflour.
- Baking soda is bicarbonate of soda.
- Vanilla or vanilla extract is vanilla essence.
- Green, red, or yellow sweet peppers are capsicums or bell peppers.
- Golden raisins are sultanas.

VOLUME AND WEIGHT

The United States traditionally uses cup measures for liquid and solid ingredients. The chart, top right, shows the approximate imperial and metric equivalents. If you are accustomed to weighing solid ingredients, the following approximate equivalents will be helpful.

- 1 cup butter, castor sugar, or rice = 8 ounces = ½ pound = 250 grams
- 1 cup flour = 4 ounces = ¼ pound = 125 grams
- 1 cup icing sugar = 5 ounces = 150 grams

Canadian and U.S. volume for a cup measure is 8 fluid ounces (237 ml), but the standard metric equivalent is 250 ml.

1 British imperial cup is 10 fluid ounces.

In Australia, 1 tablespoon equals 20 ml, and there are 4 teaspoons in the Australian tablespoon.

Spoon measures are used for smaller amounts of ingredients. Although the size of the tablespoon varies slightly in different countries, for practical purposes and for recipes in this book, a straight substitution is all that's necessary. Measurements made using cups or spoons always should be level unless stated otherwise.

COMMON WEIGHT RANGE REPLACEMENTS

Imperial / U.S.	Metric
½ ounce	15 g
1 ounce	25 g or 30 g
4 ounces (¼ pound)	115 g or 125 g
8 ounces (½ pound)	225 g or 250 g
16 ounces (1 pound)	450 g or 500 g
1¼ pounds	625 g
1½ pounds	750 g
2 pounds or 2¼ pounds	1,000 g or 1 Kg

OVEN TEMPERATURE EQUIVALENTS

Fahrenheit Setting	Celsius Setting*	Gas Setting
300°F	150°C	Gas Mark 2 (very low)
325°F	160°C	Gas Mark 3 (low)
350°F	180°C	Gas Mark 4 (moderate)
375°F	190°C	Gas Mark 5 (moderate)
400°F	200°C	Gas Mark 6 (hot)
425°F	220°C	Gas Mark 7 (hot)
450°F	230°C	Gas Mark 8 (very hot)
475°F	240°C	Gas Mark 9 (very hot)
500°F	260°C	Gas Mark 10 (extremely hot)
Broil	Broil	Grill

*Electric and gas ovens may be calibrated using celsius. However, for an electric oven, increase celsius setting 10 to 20 degrees when cooking above 160°C. For convection or forced air ovens (gas or electric) lower the temperature setting 25°F/10°C when cooking at all heat levels.

BAKING PAN SIZES

Imperial / U.S.	Metric
9×1½-inch round cake pan	22- or 23×4-cm (1.5 L)
9×1½-inch pie plate	22- or 23×4-cm (1 L)
8×8×2-inch square cake pan	20×5-cm (2 L)
9×9×2-inch square cake pan	22- or 23×4.5-cm (2.5 L)
11×7×1½-inch baking pan	28×17×4-cm (2 L)
2-quart rectangular baking pan	30×19×4.5-cm (3 L)
13×9×2-inch baking pan	34×22×4.5-cm (3.5 L)
15×10×1-inch jelly roll pan	40×25×2-cm
9×5×3-inch loaf pan	23×13×8-cm (2 L)
2-quart casserole	2 L

U.S. / STANDARD METRIC EQUIVALENTS

⅛ teaspoon = 0.5 ml	⅓ cup = 3 fluid ounces = 75 ml
¼ teaspoon = 1 ml	½ cup = 4 fluid ounces = 125 ml
½ teaspoon = 2 ml	⅔ cup = 5 fluid ounces = 150 ml
1 teaspoon = 5 ml	¾ cup = 6 fluid ounces = 175 ml
1 tablespoon = 15 ml	1 cup = 8 fluid ounces = 250 ml
2 tablespoons = 25 ml	2 cups = 1 pint = 500 ml
¼ cup = 2 fluid ounces = 50 ml	1 quart = 1 litre

index

Note: Page references in *italics* refer to photographs.

A

Aloha Kabobs, 222
Appetizers
    Brandied Blue Cheese Bread, 25
    Calypso Shrimp Cocktail, 12
    Cedar-Planked Brie with Peach Relish, 18, *19*
    Cheddar-Bacon Loaf, 29
    Cheesy Garlic Bread on a Stick, 28
    Creamy Apricot and Onion Dip, 24
    Dijon Pork Skewers with Apple-Apricot Chutney, 16
    Eggplant Dip, 26, *27*
    Grilled Black Bean and Sweet Potato Quesadillas, 17
    Grilled Cherry Tomatoes with Garlic, 22, *23*
    Grilled Greek Bread Sticks, 32
    Grilled Parmesan Breadsticks, 32, *33*
    Grilled Yellow Peppers with Herb-Caper Sauce, 20
    Hot Ribeye Bites, *11*, 13
    Smoky Wings with Double Dippers, 14, *15*
    Tomato-Brie Potato Skins, 21
    Walnut, Onion, and Prosciutto Bruschetta, 30, *31*
Apples
    Apple-Apricot Chutney, 16
    Grilled Apple Slices, 160, *161*
    Two-Tone Coleslaw, 210, *211*
Applewood-Smoked Pork Chops, 192
Apricot-Habanero Short Ribs, 122, *123*
Apricots
    Apple-Apricot Chutney, 16
    Creamy Apricot and Onion Dip, 24
    Ham Steak Sandwiches with Apricot-Cherry Chutney, 64, *65*
Asian Apricot-Glazed Chops, 111
Asparagus
    Grilled Asparagus in Dill Butter, 227
    Salmon and Asparagus with Garden Mayonnaise, 171
Avocados
    Chicken Mole Sandwiches, 68, *69*
    Chicken Wraps with Spanish Rice, 73
    Ribeyes with Avocado Sauce, 140, *141*
    Stacked Asian-Style Grouper, 168, *169*

B

Backyard Burgers, 40, *41*
Bacon
    BLT Steak, 146
    Cheddar-Bacon Loaf, 29
    Grilled Potato Salad, *205*, 209
Baked Bean Quintet, 232, *233*
Balsamic Tomatoes, 148, *149*
Barbecued Turkey Tenderloins, 197
Basil-Cucumber Salad, 208
Beans. *See also* Black beans
    Baked Bean Quintet, 232, *233*
    Chickpea Salad, 92, *93*
    Tuna and Bean Salad, 166
Beef. *See also* Beef ribs; Beef steaks
    Backyard Burgers, 40, *41*
    Burgers with Onion Jam, 36, *37*
    Five-Spice Tri-Tip Roast with Daikon Relish, 154
    Grilled Burgers Italiano, 38
    grilling times and temperatures, 9
    Jerk Burgers with Mango Salsa, 39
    Peppered Rib Roast, 155
    Raspberry-Sesame Tri-Tip Roast, 156, *157*
    Smoked Brisket with Black Bean and Corn Salsa, 188
    Spanish Meat Loaves, 138, *139*
    Texans' Beef Brisket, 186, *187*
Beef ribs
    Apricot-Habanero Short Ribs, 122, *123*
    K.C.-Style Beef Ribs, 124
    Lone Star BBQ Ribs, 125
    Spiced and Sassy Beef Ribs, 189
Beef steaks
    Beef-Spinach Sandwiches, 54
    BLT Steak, 146
    Blue Cheese and Steak Sandwiches, 52, *53*
    Easy Steak and Potato Kabobs, 152, *153*
    Flat-Iron Steak with Balsamic Tomatoes, 148, *149*
    grilling times and temperatures, 9
    Hot Ribeye Bites, *11*, 13
    Porterhouse Steak with Chipotle Potato Hash, 144, *145*
    Ribeye Steaks with Hot-as-Heck Sauce, 143
    Ribeyes with Avocado Sauce, 140, *141*
    Roasted Garlic Steak, 142
    Sausage-and-Pepper Smothered Steak, 150
    Southwestern Steak Hero, 50, *51*
    Stuffed Steak Pinwheels, 151
    Three-Herb Steaks, *137*, 147
Beer
    Beer-Brined Pork Loin Chops, 103
    Lone Star BBQ Ribs, 125
    Spicy Beer Sauce, 186
Black beans
    Black Bean and Corn Salsa, 188
    Black Bean Burgers, 49
    Black Bean Salsa, 60
    Grilled Black Bean and Sweet Potato Quesadillas, 17
Blackened Snapper with Roasted Potatoes, 162
Black Pepper Blue Cheese Dipper, 14
BLT Steak, 146
Blue Cheese and Steak Sandwiches, 52, *53*
Brandied Blue Cheese Bread, 25
Breads
    Brandied Blue Cheese Bread, 25
    Cheddar-Bacon Loaf, 29
    Cheesy Garlic Bread on a Stick, 28
    Grilled Greek Bread Sticks, 32
    Grilled Panzanella, 213
    Grilled Parmesan Breadsticks, 32, *33*
    Walnut, Onion, and Prosciutto Bruschetta, 30, *31*
Burgers
    Backyard Burgers, 40, *41*
    Black Bean Burgers, 49
    Burgers with Onion Jam, 36, *37*
    Fish Burgers with Dilled Slaw, 48
    Glazed Turkey Burgers, 46, *47*

Burgers *(continued)*
    Grilled Burgers Italiano, 38
    Jerk Burgers with Mango Salsa, 39
    Spiced Pork Burgers with Mango Mayonnaise, 42, *43*
Butter, Cumin-Lime, 223

C

Cabbage
    Green Cabbage Slaw, 48
    Honey-Mustard Slaw, 212
    Two-Tone Coleslaw, 210, *211*
Calypso Shrimp Cocktail, 12
Caramelized Salmon with Citrus Salsa, 170
Caribbean Pork with Three-Pepper Salsa, 114, *115*
Carrots
    Moroccan-Style Carrots, 231
    Ranch-Style Carrots and Squash, 224, *225*
Cedar-Planked Brie with Peach Relish, 18, *19*
Cheddar-Bacon Loaf, 29
Cheese
    Black Pepper Blue Cheese Dipper, 14
    Blue Cheese and Steak Sandwiches, 52, *53*
    Brandied Blue Cheese Bread, 25
    Burgers with Onion Jam, 36, *37*
    Cedar-Planked Brie with Peach Relish, 18, *19*
    Cheddar-Bacon Loaf, 29
    Cheesy Garlic Bread on a Stick, 28
    Cheesy Garlic Potato Gratin, 228, *229*
    Chicken Stuffed with Spinach and Sweet Peppers, 75, *77*
    Grilled Burgers Italiano, 38
    Grilled Cheesy Potatoes, 230
    Grilled Chicken Fettuccine, 80, *81*
    Grilled Greek Bread Sticks, 32
    Grilled Italian Panini, 56, *57*
    Grilled Parmesan Breadsticks, 32, *33*
    Gruyère and Pork Sandwiches, 44, *45*
    Lemon or Parmesan Couscous, 172, *173*
    Roasted Pepper-Goat Cheese Spread, 66
    Tomato-Brie Potato Skins, 21
Cherries
    Double Cherry-Chicken Roll-Ups, 78, *79*
    Ham Steak Sandwiches with Apricot-Cherry Chutney, 64, *65*

Chicken
    Chicken Mole Sandwiches, 68, *69*
    Chicken Sandwiches with Roasted Pepper-Goat Cheese Spread, *35*, 66
    Chicken Stuffed with Spinach and Sweet Peppers, 75, *77*
    Chicken Wraps with Spanish Rice, 73
    Chili-Rubbed Drumsticks, 198, *199*
    Double Cherry-Chicken Roll-Ups, 78, *79*
    Finger-Lickin' Barbecued Chicken, 84, *85*
    Grilled Chicken Fettuccine, 80, *81*
    grilling times and temperatures, 9
    Honey-Dijon Barbecued Chicken, 88, *89*
    Mango-Lime-Sauced Chicken Thighs, 87
    Mushroom-Stuffed Chicken, 82
    Orange-Coriander Glazed Chicken, 86
    Peach-Glazed Chicken, 83
    Sesame Grilled Chicken, 90
    Smoky Wings with Double Dippers, 14, *15*
    Sweet 'n' Sticky Chicken, 194, *195*
    Zesty Curry-Lime Chicken Kabobs, 76
Chicken sausages
    Chicken Sausage Sandwiches, 67
Chickpea Salad, 92, *93*
Chile peppers
    Apricot-Habanero Short Ribs, 122, *123*
    Caribbean Pork with Three-Pepper Salsa, 114, *115*
    Chicken Mole Sandwiches, 68, *69*
    Chops in Smoky Chile Marinade, 108, *109*
    Hot Ribeye Bites, *11*, 13
    Lone Star BBQ Ribs, 125
    Ribeye Steaks with Hot-as-Heck Sauce, 143
Chili-Rubbed Drumsticks, 198, *199*
Chops in Smoky Chile Marinade, 108, *109*
Chuck Wagon Baby Back Ribs, 130, *131*
Chunky Pineapple Sauce, 202, *203*
Chutney, Apple-Apricot, 16
Chutney Spareribs, 133
Cilantro Crème Fraîche, 50
Clam Bake, 180, *181*
Coconut Milk Sauce, Grilled Shrimp in, 174
Corn
    Black Bean and Corn Salsa, 188
    Black Bean Burgers, 49
    Clam Bake, 180, *181*

Corn-Mango Salsa, 107
Corn Salad, 214, *215*
Corn-Tomato Relish, 72
Grilled Corn with Cumin-Lime Butter, 223
Mexicali Vegetable Kabobs, 220, *221*
Couscous, Lemon or Parmesan, 172, *173*
Crab Zucchini Cakes, 178
Cranberry Ketchup, Kickin', 58, *59*
Creamy Apricot and Onion Dip, 24
Cucumber Basil Salad, 208
Cumin-Lime Butter, 223

D

Daikon Relish, 154
Dijon Pork Skewers with Apple-Apricot Chutney, 16
Dips. *See also* Spreads
    Black Pepper Blue Cheese Dipper, 14
    Creamy Apricot and Onion Dip, 24
    Eggplant Dip, 26, *27*
    Spicy Pesto Ranch Dipper, 14
Double Cherry-Chicken Roll-Ups, 78, *79*
Double Peanut-Crusted Chops, *99*, 110
Double-Smoked Salmon with Horseradish Cream, 201

E

East–West Ribs, 132
Easy Steak and Potato Kabobs, 152, *153*
Eggplant Dip, 26, *27*

F

Fajitas, Turkey, 96, *97*
Fennel Pork with Orzo Risotto, 112, *113*
Finger-Lickin' Barbecued Chicken, 84, *85*
Fire-Roasted Acorn Squash, 226
Fish. *See also* Salmon
    Blackened Snapper with Roasted Potatoes, 162
    Fish Burgers with Dilled Slaw, 48
    grilling times and temperatures, 9
    Halibut with Chutney Cream Sauce, 164, *165*
    Honey Smoked Trout, 200
    Lemon-and-Dill Fish Sandwiches with Tartar Sauce, 61
    Mahi Mahi with Vegetable Slaw, 163
    Sea Bass with Wilted Greens, *159*, 167
    Stacked Asian-Style Grouper, 168, *169*
    Tropical Halibut Steaks, 202, *203*

Trout with Mushroom Stuffing, 160, *161*
Tuna and Bean Salad, 166
Five-Spice Tri-Tip Roast with Daikon Relish, 154
Flat-Iron Steak with Balsamic Tomatoes, 148, *149*

G

Game Hens with Rhubarb Barbecue Glaze, 91
Garlic
    Cheesy Garlic Bread on a Stick, 28
    Grilled Cherry Tomatoes with Garlic, 22, *23*
    Roasted Garlic Steak, 142
Glaze, Hoisin-Ginger, 132
Glazed Country Ribs, 134
Glazed Prosciutto-Wrapped Shrimp, 172, *173*
Glazed Turkey Burgers, 46, *47*
Greek Honey-Lemon Pork Chops, 100, *101*
Greek-Inspired Lamb Pockets, 55
Green Cabbage Slaw, 48
Greens. *See also* Cabbage; Spinach
    BLT Steak, 146
    Calypso Shrimp Cocktail, 12
    Raspberry-Sesame Tri-Tip Roast, 156, *157*
    Summer Strawberry Salad, 217
Grilling tips and techniques, 6–9
Grouper, Stacked Asian-Style, 168, *169*
Gruyère and Pork Sandwiches, 44, *45*

H

Halibut
    Halibut with Chutney Cream Sauce, 164, *165*
    Tropical Halibut Steaks, 202, *203*
Ham. *See also* Prosciutto
    Grilled Italian Panini, 56, *57*
    Gruyère and Pork Sandwiches, 44, *45*
    Ham Steak Sandwiches with Apricot-Cherry Chutney, 64, *65*
    Ham Steaks with Fresh Peach Chutney, 119
Herbs
    Herb-Caper Sauce, 20
    Three-Herb Steaks, *137*, 147
Hickory-Smoked Turkey, 196
Hoisin-Ginger Glaze, 132
Hoisin-Honey Ribs, Spicy, 190, *191*
Honey-Dijon Barbecued Chicken, 88, *89*
Honey-Mustard Slaw, 212
Honey Smoked Trout, 200
Horseradish Cream, 201
Hot Ribeye Bites, *11*, 13

J

Jam, Onion, 36, *37*
Jerk Burgers with Mango Salsa, 39
Jicama
    Mahi Mahi with Vegetable Slaw, 163
    Salmon Wraps with Jicama Slaw, 70, *71*

K

K.C.-Style Beef Ribs, 124
Kickin' Cranberry Ketchup, 58, *59*

L

Lamb Pockets, Greek-Inspired, 55
Lemon-and-Dill Fish Sandwiches with Tartar Sauce, 61
Lemon or Parmesan Couscous, 172, *173*
Linguine and Clams in Herbed Wine Sauce, 182, *183*
Lobster
    Clam Bake, 180, *181*
    Rock Lobster Tails, 179
Lone Star BBQ Ribs, 125

M

Mahi Mahi with Vegetable Slaw, 163
Mangoes
    Corn-Mango Salsa, 107
    Jerk Burgers with Mango Salsa, 39
    Mango-Guava BBQ Sauce, 128, *129*
    Mango-Lime-Sauced Chicken Thighs, 87
    Mango Mayonnaise, 42
Marinades, working with, 7
Mayonnaise, Mango, 42
Meat. *See also* Beef; Lamb; Pork
    grilling tips, 7
Meat Loaves, Spanish, 138, *139*
Melon-Tomato Tumble, Grilled Pork with, 116, *117*
Mexicali Vegetable Kabobs, 220, *221*
Moroccan-Style Carrots, 231
Mushrooms
    Mushroom-Stuffed Chicken, 82
    Mushroom-Stuffed Pork Chops, 104, *105*
Prosciutto Pork Kabobs, 118
Trout with Mushroom Stuffing, 160, *161*
Mustard
    Dijon Pork Skewers with Apple-Apricot Chutney, 16
    Mustard Dipping Sauce, 189
    Mustard-Glazed Ribs, 135

N

Nuts. *See* Peanuts and peanut butter; Walnuts

O

Olives
    Spanish Meat Loaves, 138, *139*
Onions
    Creamy Apricot and Onion Dip, 24
    Grilled Brats with Black Bean Salsa, 60
    Onion Jam, 36, *37*
    Red Onion Relish, 56
    Walnut, Onion, and Prosciutto Bruschetta, 30, *31*
Oranges
    Caramelized Salmon with Citrus Salsa, 170
    Cherry-Orange Sauce, 78
    Orange-Balsamic Turkey Tenderloins, 94
    Orange-Coriander Glazed Chicken, 86

P

Pancakes, Zucchini, 218, *219*
Pasta
    Fennel Pork with Orzo Risotto, 112, *113*
    Game Hens with Rhubarb Barbecue Glaze, 91
    Grilled Chicken Fettuccine, 80, *81*
    Lemon or Parmesan Couscous, 172, *173*
    Linguine and Clams in Herbed Wine Sauce, 182, *183*
    Summer Vegetable Pasta Salad, 216
Peaches
    Cedar-Planked Brie with Peach Relish, 18, *19*
    Ham Steaks with Fresh Peach Chutney, 119
Peach-Glazed Chicken, 83
Peanuts and peanut butter
    Double Peanut-Crusted Chops, *99*, 110
    Thai-Style Seafood Kabobs, 175

Peas
- Aloha Kabobs, 222
- Honey-Mustard Slaw, 212
- Summer Vegetable Pasta Salad, 216

Peppered Rib Roast, 155

Peppers. See also Chile peppers
- Caribbean Pork with Three-Pepper Salsa, 114, *115*
- Chicken Stuffed with Spinach and Sweet Peppers, *75*, 77
- Grilled Burgers Italiano, 38
- Grilled Panzanella, 213
- Grilled Yellow Peppers with Herb-Caper Sauce, 20
- Roasted Pepper-Goat Cheese Spread, 66
- Sausage-and-Pepper Smothered Steak, 150

Pesto Ranch Dipper, Spicy, 14

Pesto Topper, 40, *41*

Pineapple
- Aloha Kabobs, 222
- Caramelized Salmon with Citrus Salsa, 170
- Chunky Pineapple Sauce, 202, *203*
- Summer Strawberry Salad, 217

Pork. See also Bacon; Ham; Pork ribs; Pork sausages
- Applewood-Smoked Pork Chops, 192
- Asian Apricot-Glazed Chops, 111
- Beer-Brined Pork Loin Chops, 103
- Caribbean Pork with Three-Pepper Salsa, 114, *115*
- Chops in Smoky Chile Marinade, 108, *109*
- Dijon Pork Skewers with Apple-Apricot Chutney, 16
- Double Peanut-Crusted Chops, *99*, 110
- Fennel Pork with Orzo Risotto, 112, *113*
- Greek Honey-Lemon Pork Chops, 100, *101*
- Grilled Pork with Melon-Tomato Tumble, 116, *117*
- Grilled Yogurt-Marinated Pork Chops, 102
- grilling times and temperatures, 9
- Gruyère and Pork Sandwiches, 44, *45*
- Mushroom-Stuffed Pork Chops, 104, *105*
- Pork Chop and Potato Dinner, 106
- Pork Wraps with Corn-Tomato Relish, 72
- Prosciutto Pork Kabobs, 118
- Prosciutto-Stuffed Pork, *185,* 193
- Spiced Pork Burgers with Mango Mayonnaise, 42, *43*
- Summer Pork Chops with Corn-Mango Salsa, 107

Pork ribs
- Chuck Wagon Baby Back Ribs, 130, *131*
- Chutney Spareribs, 133
- East–West Ribs, 132
- Glazed Country Ribs, 134
- Mustard-Glazed Ribs, 135
- Reggae Baby Back Ribs, 128, *129*
- Spicy Hoisin-Honey Ribs, 190, *191*
- Thai-Coconut Ribs, 126, *127*

Pork sausages
- Bratwurst with Kickin' Cranberry Ketchup, 58, *59*
- Clam Bake, 180, *181*
- Grilled Brats with Black Bean Salsa, 60
- Grilled Burgers Italiano, 38
- Sausage-and-Pepper Smothered Steak, 150
- Turkey Breast Stuffed with Sausage, Fennel, and Figs, 95

Potatoes
- Blackened Snapper with Roasted Potatoes, 162
- Cheesy Garlic Potato Gratin, 228, *229*
- Clam Bake, 180, *181*
- Easy Steak and Potato Kabobs, 152, *153*
- Grilled Black Bean and Sweet Potato Quesadillas, 17
- Grilled Cheesy Potatoes, 230
- Grilled Potato Salad, *205,* 209
- Pork Chop and Potato Dinner, 106
- Porterhouse Steak with Chipotle Potato Hash, 144, *145*
- Tomato-Brie Potato Skins, 21

Poultry. See also Chicken; Turkey
- Game Hens with Rhubarb Barbecue Glaze, 91
- marinating, 7

Prosciutto
- Glazed Prosciutto-Wrapped Shrimp, 172, *173*
- Prosciutto Pork Kabobs, 118
- Prosciutto-Stuffed Pork, *185,* 193
- Walnut, Onion, and Prosciutto Bruschetta, 30, *31*

Q

Quesadillas, Grilled Black Bean and Sweet Potato, 17

R

Ranch-Style Carrots and Squash, 224, *225*

Raspberry-Sesame Tri-Tip Roast, 156, *157*

Red Onion Relish, 56

Reggae Baby Back Ribs, 128, *129*

Relish
- Corn-Tomato Relish, 72
- Daikon Relish, 154
- Red Onion Relish, 56

Rhubarb Barbecue Glaze, Game Hens with, 91

Ribeye Steaks with Hot-as-Heck Sauce, 143

Ribeyes with Avocado Sauce, 140, *141*

Ribs. See Beef ribs; Pork ribs

Rice, Spanish, 73

Roasted Garlic Steak, 142

Roasted Pepper-Goat Cheese Spread, 66

Rock Lobster Tails, 179

Rub, Chuck Wagon, 130

Rub, Dry, Pork, 192

S

Salads. See also Slaws
- Chickpea Salad, 92, *93*
- Corn Salad, 214, *215*
- Grilled Potato Salad, *205,* 209
- Summer Strawberry Salad, 217
- Summer Vegetable Pasta Salad, 216
- Tuna and Bean Salad, 166

Salmon
- Caramelized Salmon with Citrus Salsa, 170
- Double-Smoked Salmon with Horseradish Cream, 201
- Fish Burgers with Dilled Slaw, 48
- Salmon and Asparagus with Garden Mayonnaise, 171
- Salmon Wraps with Jicama Slaw, 70, *71*

Salsa
- Black Bean and Corn Salsa, 188
- Black Bean Salsa, 60
- Corn-Mango Salsa, 107

Sandwiches. *See also* Burgers; Wraps
- Beef-Spinach Sandwiches, 54
- Blue Cheese and Steak Sandwiches, 52, *53*
- Bratwurst with Kickin' Cranberry Ketchup, 58, *59*
- Chicken Mole Sandwiches, 68, *69*
- Chicken Sandwiches with Roasted Pepper-Goat Cheese Spread, *35*, 66
- Chicken Sausage Sandwiches, 67
- Greek-Inspired Lamb Pockets, 55
- Grilled Brats with Black Bean Salsa, 60
- Grilled Italian Panini, 56, *57*
- Gruyère and Pork Sandwiches, 44, *45*
- Ham Steak Sandwiches with Apricot-Cherry Chutney, 64, *65*
- Lemon-and-Dill Fish Sandwiches with Tartar Sauce, 61
- Shrimp Po'Boy with Dried Tomato Aioli, 62, *63*
- Southwestern Steak Hero, 50, *51*

Sauces. *See also* Salsa
- Cherry-Orange Sauce, 78
- Chunky Pineapple Sauce, 202, *203*
- Herb-Caper Sauce, 20
- Horseradish Cream, 201
- Mango-Guava BBQ Sauce, 128, *129*
- Mustard Dipping Sauce, 189
- Spicy Beer Sauce, 186
- Sweet 'n' Sticky Barbecue Sauce, 194
- Tartar Sauce, 61
- Tomato-Sour Cream Sauce, 178
- Vinegar Mop Sauce, 186

Sausages. *See* Chicken sausages; Pork sausages

Scallops
- grilling times and temperatures, 9
- Soy-Lime Scallops with Leeks, 176, *177*
- Thai-Style Seafood Kabobs, 175

Sea Bass with Wilted Greens, *159*, 167
Sesame Grilled Chicken, 90
Sesame-Raspberry Tri-Tip Roast, 156, *157*

Shellfish. *See also* Shrimp
- Clam Bake, 180, *181*
- grilling times and temperatures, 9
- Linguine and Clams in Herbed Wine Sauce, 182, *183*
- Rock Lobster Tails, 179
- Soy-Lime Scallops with Leeks, 176, *177*
- Thai-Style Seafood Kabobs, 175
- Zucchini Crab Cakes, 178

Shrimp
- Calypso Shrimp Cocktail, 12
- Glazed Prosciutto-Wrapped Shrimp, 172, *173*
- Grilled Shrimp in Coconut Milk Sauce, 174
- grilling times and temperatures, 9
- Shrimp Po'Boy with Dried Tomato Aioli, 62, *63*
- Thai-Style Seafood Kabobs, 175

Slaws
- Green Cabbage Slaw, 48
- Honey-Mustard Slaw, 212
- Two-Tone Coleslaw, 210, *211*

Smoked Brisket with Black Bean and Corn Salsa, 188
Smoky Wings with Double Dippers, 14, *15*
Snapper, Blackened, with Roasted Potatoes, 162
Southwestern Steak Hero, 50, *51*
Soy-Lime Scallops with Leeks, 176, *177*
Spanish Meat Loaves, 138, *139*
Spanish Rice, 73
Spiced and Sassy Beef Ribs, 189
Spiced Pork Burgers with Mango Mayonnaise, 42, *43*
Spicy Beer Sauce, 186
Spicy Hoisin-Honey Ribs, 190, *191*
Spicy Pesto Ranch Dipper, 14

Spinach
- Beef-Spinach Sandwiches, 54
- Chicken Stuffed with Spinach and Sweet Peppers, *75*, 77
- Prosciutto-Stuffed Pork, *185*, 193
- Sea Bass with Wilted Greens, *159*, 167
- Stuffed Steak Pinwheels, 151

Spreads
- Cilantro Crème Fraîche, 50
- Kickin' Cranberry Ketchup, 58, *59*
- Onion Jam, 36, *37*
- Pesto Topper, 40, *41*
- Roasted Pepper-Goat Cheese Spread, 66
- Squished Tomato Topper, 40, *41*

Squash. *See also* Zucchini
- Chicken Sausage Sandwiches, 67
- Fire-Roasted Acorn Squash, 226
- Ranch-Style Carrots and Squash, 224, *225*
- Tomato-Squash Salad, 206, *207*

Squished Tomato Topper, 40, *41*
Stacked Asian-Style Grouper, 168, *169*
Strawberry Salad, Summer, 217
Stuffed Steak Pinwheels, 151
Summer Pork Chops with Corn-Mango Salsa, 107
Summer Strawberry Salad, 217
Summer Vegetable Pasta Salad, 216
Sweet 'n' Sticky Barbecue Sauce, 194
Sweet 'n' Sticky Chicken, 194, *195*
Sweet Potato and Black Bean Quesadillas, Grilled, 17

T

Tahini Turkey Thighs, 92, *93*
Tartar Sauce, 61
Texans' Beef Brisket, 186, *187*
Thai-Coconut Ribs, 126, *127*
Thai-Style Seafood Kabobs, 175
Three-Herb Steaks, *137*, 147

Tomatoes
- Balsamic Tomatoes, 148, *149*
- BLT Steak, 146
- Calypso Shrimp Cocktail, 12
- Corn-Tomato Relish, 72
- Grilled Cherry Tomatoes with Garlic, 22, *23*
- Grilled Panzanella, 213
- Grilled Pork with Melon-Tomato Tumble, 116, *117*
- Spicy Beer Sauce, 186
- Squished Tomato Topper, 40, *41*
- Stacked Asian-Style Grouper, 168, *169*
- Summer Vegetable Pasta Salad, 216
- Tomato-Brie Potato Skins, 21
- Tomato-Sour Cream Sauce, 178
- Tomato-Squash Salad, 206, *207*

Tortillas. *See also* Wraps
- Grilled Black Bean and Sweet Potato Quesadillas, 17
- Turkey Fajitas, 96, *97*

Tropical Halibut Steaks, 202, *203*

Trout
- Honey Smoked Trout, 200
- Trout with Mushroom Stuffing, 160, *161*

Tuna
- Fish Burgers with Dilled Slaw, 48
- Tuna and Bean Salad, 166

Turkey
- Barbecued Turkey Tenderloins, 197
- Glazed Turkey Burgers, 46, *47*
- grilling times and temperatures, 9

Turkey *(continued)*
    Hickory-Smoked Turkey, 196
    Orange-Balsamic Turkey Tenderloins, 94
    Tahini Turkey Thighs, 92, *93*
    Turkey Breast Stuffed with Sausage, Fennel, and Figs, 95
    Turkey Fajitas, 96, *97*
Two-Tone Coleslaw, 210, *211*

V

Vinegar Mop Sauce, 186

W

Walnuts
    Black Bean Burger, 49
    Walnut, Onion, and Prosciutto Bruschetta, 30, *31*
Wraps
    Chicken Wraps with Spanish Rice, 73
    Pork Wraps with Corn-Tomato Relish, 72
    Salmon Wraps with Jicama Slaw, 70, *71*

Z

Zesty Curry-Lime Chicken Kabobs, 76
Zucchini
    Mexicali Vegetable Kabobs, 220, *221*
    Prosciutto Pork Kabobs, 118
    Summer Vegetable Pasta Salad, 216
    Turkey Fajitas, 96, *97*
    Zesty Curry-Lime Chicken Kabobs, 76
    Zucchini Crab Cakes, 178
    Zucchini Pancakes, 218, *219*